THE HEART OF

LIBRARIANSHIP

ALA Editions purchases fund advocacy, awareness, and accreditation programs for library professionals worldwide.

THE HEART OF

LIBRARIANSHIP

ATTENTIVE, POSITIVE, AND PURPOSEFUL CHANGE

MICHAEL STEPHENS

AN IMPRINT OF THE AMERICAN LIBRARY ASSOCIATION
CHICAGO | 2016

MICHAEL STEPHENS is assistant professor in the School of Information at San José State University. He has consulted and presented for U.S. embassies in Germany, Switzerland, and Turkey, and presents to both national and international audiences about emerging technologies, learning, innovation, and libraries. Since 2010 Stephens has written the monthly column "Office Hours" for *Library Journal* exploring the issues, ideas, and emerging trends in libraries and LIS education. To review Stephens's archive of work, visit his Tame the Web website and blog http://tametheweb.com.

ISBNs
978-0-8389-1454-0 (paper)
978-0-8389-1464-9 (PDF)
978-0-8389-1465-6 (ePub)
978-0-8389-1466-3 (Kindle)

Library of Congress Cataloging-in-Publication Data
Names: Stephens, Michael T., 1965– author.
Title: The heart of librarianship : attentive, positive, and purposeful change / Michael Stephens.
Description: Chicago : ALA Editions, an imprint of the American Library Association, 2016. | Includes essays from Michael Stephens's Library journal "Office Hours" columns. | Includes bibliographical references and index.
Identifiers: LCCN 2016006592 | ISBN 9780838914540 (paperback)
Subjects: LCSH: Library science—Philosophy. | Library science—Forecasting. | Libraries and community. | Libraries—Technological innovations. | Library education. | Librarians—Professional relationships.
Classification: LCC Z665 .S746 2016 | DDC 020–dc23 LC record available at https://lccn.loc.gov/2016006592

Cover design by Alejandra Diaz. Imagery © Shutterstock, Inc. Text design and composition by Pauline Neuwirth in the ITC New Baskerville Std, Steelfish, and Helvetica Neue LT Std typefaces.

♾ This paper meets the requirements of ANSI/NISO Z39.48–1992 (Permanence of Paper).

Printed in the United States of America
20 19 18 17 16   5 4 3 2 1

CONTENTS

6 INFINITE LEARNING

Library Learning, Collaboration, Support, Professional Development

FOREWORD

WE COULD BE living in the age of empathy. Or at least the age when empathy—defined by *Psychology Today* as "the experience of understanding another person's condition from their perspective"—is getting some fabulous press, if perhaps not a whole lot of practice.[1]

One of empathy's major cheerleaders is none other than President Barack Obama, who's espoused the benefits of empathy—and decried the "empathy deficit"—from campaign speeches to commencement addresses, even controversially citing empathy as one of the criteria for Supreme Court justices.[2]

Publishing has helped draw attention to empathy with a steady parade of books, including Jeremy Rifkin's *The Empathic Civilization* (there's a Ted Talk), which positions a growth in empathy as the only solution to our many technology-induced problems—and my favorite—Roman Krznaric's *Empathy: Why It Matters, and How to Get It*, which calls on us to regenerate our empathy through six practices.[3] For Krznaric, exercising empathy will not only make us more creative and happier, it will also lead to a more just society.

To seal the deal, empathy has even received the blessing of science. Mirror neurons, it turns out, provide a neuroscience-based explanation for why the same parts of the brain "fire" whether we are actually experiencing an action—dropping a freshly scooped ice cream cone—or merely observing someone engaged in the same misfortune.[4]

Heads up, librarians! If this all sounds a bit remote, some recent research points to reading literary fiction as having the ability, according to psychologist Raymond Mar, to place you squarely in the character's shoes, giving rise to the headline, "How Literature Inspires Empathy." [5] Nice to get science's acknowledgment, but could any reader have really thought otherwise after spending a weekend with Madame Bovary?

Empathy isn't just a faddish notion getting play in the popular literature. The age of empathy is having a real impact on medicine, nursing, and the other helping professions, like social work. The Internet is awash in research, studies, and reports on why doctors lose empathy, how to (or can you?) teach them empathy, and how empathetic doctors have patients with better results.

But search for "librarians and empathy" and you won't find much. Yes, there's an occasional mention of it in discussing the arcane "reference interview," a clinical term that is quick to suck any empathy out of an otherwise human conversation. In fact, librarians, I would argue, have always had trouble with empathy, often equating professionalism with the ability to keep your users at a distance, never mind walking in their shoes.

Which is why, of course, I love the writing of Michael Stephens. While the "E word" only makes an appearance a few times, his writing, indeed his worldview, is imbued with empathy. It informs his perspective as a professor: "As a teacher, I practice radical trust. I will never look over shoulders and scold a student for peeking at e-mail or the score of the big game, or practice scare tactics to make sure they do the assigned readings. They're adults." In creating library services, he flips us from planning for ourselves to empathizing with our public: "When a librarian asks me how to figure out what new services, tech, or materials to provide, I'll always start with 'ask your users.'"

Empathy is key in collaboration, how we work today: "Understanding and empathy among cross-cultural partners in a technological environment is key to success. Technology doesn't solve our problems, but it can be a conduit to making change and promoting progress." It's also an important skill that library and information science (LIS) educators must cultivate in their students: "You must be a people person in today's library. Empathic listening goes hand in hand with acceptance."

While full of tales of innovation, ideas that challenge our practice, and a regular dose of critical thinking, these pages are likewise full of humanism and heart. Quoting a participant at a conference, Stephens writes: "Participation occurs when someone welcomed as a guest feels as though they have become a host." I would rewrite that to read: participation occurs when someone experiences empathy and feels as though they can now empathize with others.

I think that all readers of *The Heart of Librarianship* will experience this gift of empathy from Stephens, and will, I hope, hand in hand with our communities, go out and create the libraries for our future.

Brian Kenney

NOTES

1. *Psychology Today,* https://www.psychologytoday.com/basics/empathy.
2. Mark Honigsbaum, "Barack Obama and the 'Empathy Deficit,'" *The Guardian,* January 4, 2013, www.theguardian.com/science/2013/jan/04/barack-obama-empathy-deficit.
3. Jeremy Rifkin, *The Empathic Civilization* (New York: TarcherPerigree, 2009), https://www.ted.com/talks/jeremy_rifkin_on_the_empathic_civilization; Roman Krznaric, *Empathy: Why It Matters, and How to Get It* (New York: TarcherPerigree, 2014).
4. Marco Iacoboni, "Imitation, Empathy, and Mirror Neurons," *Annual Review of Psychology* 60 (2009): 653–70.
5. Raymond A. Mar, Keith Oatley, and Jordan B. Peterson, "Exploring the Link between Reading Fiction and Empathy: Ruling Out Individual Differences and Examining Outcomes," *Communications* 34, no. 4 (2009): 407–28.

PREFACE

I FEEL FORTUNATE. Fortunate to have found my way to public library work in 1991, fortunate to have discovered the wonders of the Internet and World Wide Web with the incredible librarians at the St. Joseph County Public Library (South Bend, Indiana) throughout the 1990s and 2000s, and fortunate to have found an online community via blogging and various other networks over the years where sharing and collaboration know no boundaries.

I have also traveled a lot over the past twelve years or so, speaking at conferences, teaching workshops, and conducting research. I joke that I've been asked to "run my mouth" in a lot of wonderful places, but truth be told I approach each trip as a way to tap into the mindset of library folk everywhere. I have learned valuable lessons about our work from librarians all over the world.

Drawing from these meetings and conversations, I shared my insights in articles and my "Office Hours" column in *Library Journal*. A charmed hour at a *Stammtisch* (regular get-together) in Berlin with library and museum professionals sharing concerns and successes. A deeply reflective group experience in the mountains of Colorado challenging the nature of what we do through the lens of risk and reward. These and other experiences have influenced and informed my writing and teaching. Like revisiting a favorite story or song, the "Office Hours" columns of mine collected in this book capture moments in time when I gained insight about the profession.

Preparing this collection has given me time to reflect on our practice. For me, the heart of librarianship is learning. It's a cyclical process of support, engagement, and discovery with deep roots in the concepts of service, access, and freedom to pursue interests of all kinds. No matter what type of institution, someone is gaining knowledge, finding information, or creating something new based on our facilitation. And in my opinion, the role of facilitator and guide is best delivered with humanity and heart.

Libraries encourage the heart, which means we should lead from the heart, learn from the heart, and play from the heart. It means we are all-in all the time, not just when it's convenient. It means bucking the status quo to do the right thing at the right moment. It means owning our actions as professionals. It means creating institutions that expand minds and craft futures.

ACKNOWLEDGMENTS

SPECIAL THANKS TO these folks for their guidance and editorial expertise:

Francine Fialkoff, Josh Hadro, and Meredith Schwartz at
Library Journal
Emily S. Darowski, San José State University School of
Information
Patrick Hogan, ALA Editions

And I wish to personally thank the following people for their contributions to my learning, inspiration, and knowledge in creating this book:

Stephen Abram

John Blyberg

Erik Boekesteijn

Char Booth

Peter Bromberg

Michael Casey

Sean Casserly

Warren Cheetham

Kathryn Deiss

Martin Garnar

Justin Hoenke

Jan Holmquist

Kyle Jones

Brian Kenney

Stacie Ledden

Jenny Levine

Brian O'Connor

Aaron Schmidt

Karen Schneider

Jaap Van de Geer

Jessamyn West

THE HYPERLINKED LIBRARIAN

Skills, Mind-Sets, and Ideas for
Working in the Evolving Library

"THE WEB HAS changed everything." A simple statement but so indicative of how the world has evolved with emerging mechanisms for global communication and collaboration. I've used this statement in slide decks and in my teaching. It has also become an integral part of an evolving model of library services focused on user-centric opportunities to engage and learn, capitalizing on the affordances of network-enabled technologies.

The hyperlinked library model is synthesized from data collected on emerging societal trends, socio-technological research reports from Pew Internet and American Life, OCLC, EDUCAUSE, and the writings of such authors as Henry Jenkins, David Weinberger, Clay Shirky, Douglas Thomas, John Seely Brown, and Seth Godin. My model for the "hyperlinked library" is born out of the ongoing evolution of libraries and library services. Weinberger's chapter "The Hyperlinked Organization" in *The Cluetrain Manifesto* was a foundational resource for defining this model.[1] I've been writing and presenting about it for a few years around the United States and abroad—expanding and augmenting as emerging ideas and technologies take libraries in unforeseen directions. The evolving library is not a new idea—we've been talking about it for years. "The Library is unlimited and cyclical" is just as powerful today as it was when Jorge Luis Borges wrote it in "The Library of Babel" in 1941.[2]

Hyperlinked library practice is based on the ideas, concepts, and trends of our socio-technological landscape. The hyperlinked librarian understands the following:

- The library is everywhere—it is not just the building or virtual spaces.
- Hyperlinking subverts existing organizational structures.
- Our institutions should be flatter and team-based.
- Seamless service should be available across all channels of interaction.
- We must reach all users, not just those who come through our doors.
- The most powerful information services to date are probably found in the palm of everyone's hand.
- The path forward will always be an evolutionary one.
- Inevitably, there will always be some amount of chaos.

The hyperlinked librarian uses the following methods to inform practice:

- Gathering evidence of all kinds to make decisions
- Spotting trends that impact service and changing user behavior
- Integrating the new built on a foundation of core ethics and values
- Playfully approaching opportunities to create learning experiences and engaging information-based services

We can meet change with traditional methods or more chaotic methods, or somewhere in between. Regardless, future librarians need to understand that the current environment requires handling multifaceted issues simultaneously. One way of handling change graciously is through reflective practice. As we take time to contemplate our environment and circumstances, and the decisions we make, we will be more open to new ideas and poised to take action on those ideas.

As we seek to make change, we need to be careful and not let the status quo or the excuse of no time hold us back from progress.

Putting this into practice requires consideration and reflection. The following essays explore these ideas for the skill sets and paradigms required for evolving library service. Although changing the status quo is difficult, our libraries must evolve to meet user preferences.

Above all, librarians entering the hyperlinked arena must be curious and creative.

NOTES

1. Rick Levine, Christopher Locke, Doc Searls, and David Weinberger, *The Cluetrain Manifesto: The End of Business as Usual* (New York: Basic Books, 2001).
2. Jorge Luis Borges, "The Library of Babel," 1941, www.sjsu.edu/faculty/harris/ DigLit_F10/Readings/Borges%20Babel.pdf.

HERETICAL THOUGHTS

DURING A PHONE conversation with a valued colleague who runs a university library, we discussed the process of hiring. My colleague described working hard to streamline staffing and budgets owing to a financial shortfall, while holding steady to a strategic plan anchored in creating useful information and collaboration spaces for the student body. I asked the question I always ask when I'm talking to someone who hires new librarians: "What non-traditional skills and competencies should a new librarian have?" His response? "I want risk-takers . . . innovators . . . creatives . . . I don't want someone who's afraid to make a move or make a decision without getting permission." We chatted longer about skills that are becoming more important, usurping some of our long-standing curricular mainstays. Afterward, I continued to think about these skills and how they can be taught.

STRATEGIC THINKING AND PLANNING

As budgets fall and library use rises, LIS students need a solid foundation in project management and planning. I honestly can't recall too much devoted to strategic, technology, or long-range planning in my own graduate work. I do remember watching reference books being wheeled into the classroom and explained one by one. That class time would have been better spent developing a mock plan for phasing out part of our print reference and the ins and outs of acquiring, leasing, and paying for online resources.

Programs drawn from schools of business and public administration would be a good fit for the soon-to-be-librarian. Our students need grounding in concepts like decision-making, advocacy, human resources, administration, and management of nonprofits. As staffing structures change, like in the example of my colleague, a newly hired librarian may be called upon to take over departments or projects.

How do we LIS educators—and others—create pragmatic projects to reinforce these important abilities? In my classes, the dreaded group project becomes a real-world example. Here's an intriguing assignment for students: give a group a plan that was halted midstream, with directions to pick up the pieces and "make it work"—complete with roadblocks from administrators above and front-line staff below.

CREATIVITY AND INNOVATION

Thinking and planning are important but so is innovation and creativity. I've used Daniel Pink's *A Whole New Mind* in my introduction to LIS classes to highlight the importance of right-brain thinking.[1] Pink argues that the logically focused left brain, though necessary in professional work, has given way to the more artistic and conceptual right brain. Creative work is what remains after outsourcing and turning repetitive work over to computers.

Pink also stresses the importance of empathy and the power of story to transform products and services.[2] Solutions to common problems can come when librarians tap into their creativity and inventiveness. For example, we could create and deliver library services built on human emotion that add to the ongoing story of a community, as they are doing at the DOK Library's Agora in Delft, The Netherlands.[3] Agora is a multimedia center where patrons can craft personal stories using provided space and software, and then broadcast those stories on one of many screens on a 33' × 10' video wall. The exhibits focus on a community-driven theme and change periodically. Clearly, this project was born out of creativity and interest in the library user.

Not all students are immediately ready to take this on. Some can only operate within the constraints of their own limited assumptions of what library work is. However, we can build greater creativity through our instruction practices. To conclude one semester, my introduction to LIS students walked a local labyrinth, as Pink describes, to engage the left brain and free the right to explore new ideas. "Think about your professional practice," I said before the walk. "What can you do to encourage the heart of your library users?"

I caught up with one of the students from that class, Tara Wood, and asked her what she thought about it. "I think that it is just as easy for students to fall into a certain 'comfort zone' as it is for librarians. We get used to coming to class, listening to lectures, writing papers, etc., but these are not always the best methods for learning. At first, we all felt a little silly walking the labyrinth, but by the end we felt differently. . . . [I felt] a sense of clearing out the 'junk' in my mind and being able to focus."

FOCUS ON THE HEART

As a teacher, I practice radical trust. I will never look over shoulders and scold a student for peeking at e-mail or the score of the big game, or practice scare tactics to make sure they do the assigned readings. They're adults. In exploring the idea of fear as a mechanism for learning, Seth Godin writes in *Linchpin* that instead of "fear-based, test-based battlefields, [classrooms] could so easily be organized to encourage the heretical thought we so badly need."[4] As my colleague agreed, heretical thought may be the quality of choice for future employers.

Personally, I don't want students to memorize facts. I never give exams and focus instead on writing and personal reflection about the practice of librarianship. I find the strongest student papers are usually those with a personal slant that tell a story as a means to show comprehension of course material. I want LIS students to understand what it means to be in the ultimate service profession. Being a good, innovative librarian means taking a humanistic stance toward policy, decision-making, and experimentation. It means focusing on the heart.

NOTES

1. Daniel H. Pink, *A Whole New Mind: Why Right-Brainers Will Rule the Future* (New York: Penguin, 2006).
2. Ibid.
3. Erik Boekesteijn, "What's Your Story? Dutch Library DOK's New Cutting-Edge Community Tech Projects," *Library Journal,* September 1, 2010, http://lj.libraryjournal.com/2010/09/technology/whats-your-story-dutch-library-doks-new-cutting-edge-community-tech-projects/#_.
4. Seth Godin, *Linchpin: Are You Indispensable? How to Drive Your Career and Create a Remarkable Future* (New York: Portfolio, 2010), 44.

CAN WE HANDLE THE TRUTH?

IF YOU HAVEN'T read the 2010 *Project Information Literacy Progress Report* from Alison J. Head and Michael B. Eisenberg, you should.[1] "Truth Be Told: How College Students Evaluate and Use Information in the Digital Age" is for anyone who plans for or serves the needs of students of higher education. Published by the iSchool at the University of Washington and funded by the MacArthur Foundation, the report is valuable for public and school librarians, too. The traits of the information consumers studied here are those of your users or potential users. The authors note that research is daunting for college students. They first turn for help to instructors, classmates, and friends or family, not librarians.

A WAKE-UP CALL

Some of the specific findings should galvanize all of us. On the research process: "Students relied on librarians infrequently, if ever, whether they were conducting research for coursework or for personal use. Moreover, students . . . [used] librarians less often than they reported in the 2009 survey results."[2] On evaluating resources: "Few students in the sample asked librarians (11%) or writing center staff (7%) for help . . . and even fewer turned to librarians for help evaluating information for personal use (5%)."[3] On information-seeking for personal needs: "70% of this year's sample of students frequently turned to social networks, such as Facebook . . . in their daily lives."[4]

Ultimately, the authors of the report make a series of recommendations, including a few that librarians must heed. "We believe library instruction could benefit from some serious rethinking and re-examination. We recommend modifying sessions (in-class and reference encounters) so they emphasize . . . framing a successful research process . . . over research-finding of sources."[5] Librarians' focus on sources over teaching the research process itself has probably contributed to these disheartening survey results. But they also make me wonder how most college students see librarians. Are they invisible within their libraries and academic departments? Ineffective in bibliographic instruction sessions? (Just typing "bibliographic instruction sessions" makes my eyes glaze over.)

These findings complement those reported by Ithaka in 2013, which state that university researchers are relying less and less on the services of libraries and librarians and more on specific online resources.[6] What role will academic librarians play in the lives of students as well as these faculty who view the library as less and less of a partner? In a phone conversation, university librarian Jeffrey G. Trzeciak at McMaster University in Hamilton, Ontario, told me he believes "librarians have lost their audience already. . . . They will likely never come back." His gloomy words should be a rallying cry for all university and college librarians and to LIS education as well.

CHANGE WE CAN EMBRACE

There may be an antidote to this grim news. Here are some proposals:

End the disconnect between some LIS schools and the libraries in their institutions. Instead, LIS schools should partner with their institutions' libraries to form learning laboratories. Professors, librarians, and students must work together to create new models of service and outreach. These models are evaluated and tweaked, and effective practice is reported to the greater community.

Replace "bibliographic instruction" with multichannel delivery (in person, online, at the point of need) of the basics and advanced steps for research. LIS students should learn fewer "subject of the week" resources and focus more on process, critical thinking, and workflow. It's not just about "five databases for finding articles" but social networks and alternative information streams as well.

Increase the value of students' own personal learning network—they probably have one and don't even know it. Use Facebook and other info streams to match up similarly focused undergrads and grads to enhance their learning and sharing—and feed into the research process.

Expand liaison programs, where the librarian is housed in the discipline's school—visible, vocal, and active with faculty. While much current LIS education can prepare people for this, these embedded librarians will also need other skills focused on communication, the specific discipline, and research methods and support.

Make the library building itself the Commons—as per Georgia Tech and Loyola—where support, technology, and space inspire student creativity.[7] LIS schools must offer coursework devoted to planning, implementing, and evaluating the Commons both physically and virtually.

Overall, we need to handle these truths. The solutions above will clearly move us in the right direction. Only then will libraries/librarians avoid fading into the background and increase visibility in ways that may surprise our students and our faculty.

NOTES

1. Alison J. Head and Michael B. Eisenberg, "Truth Be Told: How College Students Evaluate and Use Information in the Digital Age," *Project Information Literacy Progress Report*, November 1, 2010, http://projectinfolit.org/images/pdfs/pil_fa112010_survey_fullreport1.pdf.
2. Ibid., 8.
3. Ibid., 13.

4. Ibid., 40.
5. Ibid., 39.
6. Ross Housewright, Roger C. Schonfeld, and Kate Wulfson, "Ithaka S+R US Faculty Survey 2012," *Ithaka S+R,* April 8, 2013, www.sr.ithaka.org/wp-content/uploads/2015/08/Ithaka_SR_US_Faculty_Survey_2012_FINAL.pdf.
7. Library Commons, http://librarycommons.gatech.edu; www.luc.edu/ic/.

HOLDING US BACK

WHAT IS HOLDING LIBRARIANS BACK?

This question is from a friend who has done great work in the museum field. During one conversation, we pondered what's preventing many libraries from ramping up community engagement and user-focused services. I argued for a few factors: in some places (not all) there's a lingering emphasis on collections over users, a lack of a future focus by administrators, a lack of public awareness, and, frankly, confusion on how to go forward into a landscape that seems new and frightening.

SERVICES IN MIND

A 2013 report from the Pew Research Center's Internet & American Life Project, "Library Services in the Digital Age," sheds light on what library patrons want.[1] It summarizes findings from a survey asking Americans over the age of sixteen what existing library services they like and what new services they would like to see. Such reports should be required reading for all in LIS education, especially those involved in strategic and long-range planning. They are a call to action for reevaluating core and elective course content so that library professionals are better prepared to enter the workforce and build programs and services that meet patron needs.

Regarding technology, the Pew report indicated that a "notable share" of respondents would like to see more services such as app-based access to collections, the ability to test-run devices in a "technology petting zoo," and "Redbox"-like kiosks located throughout the community that disperse library materials.[2] Around 60–70 percent of the respondents indicated they would be "very likely" or "somewhat likely" to use these and other innovative technologies. This is a big deal, and those services absolutely merit discussion. The study also notes that people use the library website to search the catalog and find basic library information, even as library web presence promotion is lacking. "When I receive the e-mails, they never reference the website," writes one user. "I didn't even know they had a website."[3] Another intriguing fact: respondents want the library to use the channels they use—Facebook and e-mail, specifically. What's not surprising: no respondent mentioned Quick Response codes, those smartphone-readable, bar code-style squares that for a few months librarians put on *everything*.

Meanwhile, the description of libraries as "book warehouses" is giving way in many communities as collections evolve and space is at a premium. Users and library staff alike broadly agreed that moving collections out to make room is a good thing, though some librarians expressed concerns. Positive statements, such as this from a librarian—"We don't have space to waste on things people don't use. It's not about us—it's about the community"—emphasize the user direction that should illuminate planning for the future.[4] In terms of current viewpoints and future ideas, quotes from library staff are likewise revealing: "The administration is overly hesitant to make any changes to services, even small ones, for fear of repercussions for other branches in the library district."[5]

REACHING OUT

It's easy to focus on the folks who use our services consistently, the ones who borrow materials, attend programs, and bring children to story time. However, the next step I would call "radical community engagement," and it begins with statements like this: "I think our strength is in our ties to the community and the relationships we build with our customers. That should be our focus and should drive how we develop our programs and services in the future." Golden! The need to be vocal can't be overemphasized: "We need to change the concept of the library as a restricted, quiet space—we bustle, we rock, we engage, but so many people in the community do not know this." The Pew report is evidence that tapping in to community needs and interests is paramount for libraries, and active interaction with citizens, businesses, nonprofits, and other entities will yield a promising future. Open the doors to local experts and creators to teach and share.

MORE THAN TEACHING

Take a look at the "About" page for the 4th Floor project at the Chattanooga Public Library.[6] "While traditional library spaces support the consumption of knowledge by offering access to media, the 4th Floor is unique because it supports the production, connection, and sharing of knowledge by offering access to tools and instruction." This exemplifies the potential of thinking beyond collections to a library space that promotes creativity and collaborative learning. Just as the Chicago Public Library's YOUmedia space has inspired similar spaces, the 4th Floor will set a standard for the next evolution of what we consider a library.[7]

As I've mentioned already, Daniel Pink, in *A Whole New Mind*, talks about focusing on creativity and empathy and how those who think with the right brain will "rule this century."[8] I think it's the converse mind-set that's holding us back. This quote from the survey scares me the most: "If I had wanted to teach people how to make stuff, I would have been a teacher. I think libraries are more about helping people learn for themselves."[9] That's certainly not the mindset we want coming out of library school or guiding our libraries. We should be able to say, "We teach, we develop independent learning skills, we inspire, and so much more!" If we can teach our students about these new things, but they enter a workplace culture that doesn't support transformation, their skills will go to waste. Thus, librarians should seek to encourage and facilitate learning of all kinds within our spaces.

NOTES

1. Kathryn Zickuhr, Lee Rainie, and Kristen Purcell, "Library Services in the Digital Age," Pew Research Center's Internet & American Life Project, January 22, 2013, http://libraries.pewinternet.org/files/legacy-pdf/PIP_Library%20 services_Report.pdf.
2. Ibid., 3.
3. Ibid., 28.
4. Ibid., 56.
5. Ibid., 73.
6. "About 4th Floor," Chattanooga Public Library, http://chattlibrary.org/content/4th-floor/about-4th-floor.
7. "Youth Media Chicago: Youth-Powered 21st Century Learning," Youth Media Chicago, http://youmediachicago.org/.
8. Daniel H. Pink, *A Whole New Mind: Why Right-Brainers Will Rule the Future* (New York: Penguin, 2006).
9. Zickuhr, Rainie, and Purcell, "Library Services in the Digital Age," http://libraries.pewinternet.org/files/legacy-pdf/PIP_Library%20services_Report.pdf, 74.

ALWAYS DOESN'T LIVE HERE ANYMORE

SOME OF THE most creative and flexible librarians I know have been working for more than a few years in libraries. Some of the most inspiring and influential professionals in our field have had distinguished careers and still continue to make a mark on our governance and future. I was lucky to learn about collection development, reference service, and weeding during my public library days from professionals who had worked in the system for multiple decades. These are the same folks who did not shy away from the Internet and its capabilities in the mid-1990s.

WE'VE ALWAYS DONE IT THIS WAY

That said, I must comment on some threads of conversation I had at one Annual Conference (ALA). In 2006 I wrote a post at Tame the Web (TTW) entitled "Five Phrases I Hope I Never Hear in Libraries Again."[1] It got a lot of traction back then, during the heyday of LIS blogging, and I used a slide of the phrases for many years in presentations. One of the phrases was: *We've always done it this way.* Back then I wrote, "I think it's time to red flag any utterance of that phrase in our libraries and make sure it's not just an excuse to avoid change. It may, however, be the best way to do something." I urged readers to explore alternatives and new ways of working to make sure efficiencies couldn't be improved. I cautioned: if librarians are hiding behind that phrase because they've had enough new things or just want to keep things the same, it might be time to move on. It has been ten years since I wrote that post. But sometimes I still have colleagues in the field say to me that they are stymied by people who "have always done it that way" and refuse to change.

Another phrase is closely linked with the above: *He/she is a road-block to getting anything done.* One colleague noted a supervisor who wouldn't implement a needed and beneficial change in processes because the person responsible for the work had been doing it the same way for thirty-five years. Another said simply, "People are waiting for her to retire." I often heard this phrase in a whisper from an exasperated librarian who can't seem to get anything done because someone on his or her team or above stopped everything in its tracks. "A proposal has been on her desk for six weeks . . . we're all waiting," said one colleague in hushed tones.

WHY WE CAN'T WAIT

In this climate of rapid change and tight budgets, we can't take six or twelve months, form a committee, write agendas, meet, transcribe the minutes, make more agendas, have more meetings, and on and on. The best librarians make good, rapid decisions based on evidence, experience, and a view of the big picture.

I recently tweeted out the link to the old TTW post. Daniel Cornwall, from the State Library of Alaska, replied, "This 2006 post is all too relevant [now]. But at least it doesn't quite seem the dominant point of view anymore. Hope?" Yes, there is hope. Perhaps these tides have turned, and even though we're still hearing of a few institutions mired in dysfunction and a lack of forward-thinking, they are no longer the norm.

NOT JUST INDIVIDUALS

I'd argue, though, that the profession as a whole suffers a bit from this. Do some association committees talk things to death? Why do some vendors we work with use the same old licensing schemes? It's safe to have endless meetings. It's safe not to disrupt the way our business works.

HOW TO CHANGE THE GAME

How can we get around these issues? Nimble and quick teams, such as Skunk Works, come to mind.[2] They are empowered to push through or around any roadblocks, fast-tracking solutions to get things done. This works best if the administration is on board. In fact, getting rid of these sentiments is easiest when the person at the top is leading the way. I recently chatted with Sean Casserly from Johnson County, Overland Park, Kansas. He had this to say:

"Understanding your organization's collective mind-set is a complex problem. If you can understand where you are and you have a general idea of the direction you want to go in and can share that vision with your staff and they believe in that vision, then you need to support them and get out of their way."

If you are currently leading a library, department, or team, I'd suggest you do the same.

Finally, if you are leading a library and have said things such as, "We've always done it this way," maybe it's time to take a long, hard look at why you are saying them. Maybe it's time to get to the root of the problem: a mind-set focused on the past, not the future.

NOTES

1. Michael Stephens, "Five Phrases I Hope I Never Hear in Libraries Again (Based on a True Story)," Tame the Web, April 9, 2006, http://tametheweb. com/2006/04/09/five-phrases-i-hope-i-never-hear-in-libraries-again-based-on-a-true-story/.
2. "Skunk Works," Lockheed Martin, www.lockheedmartin.com/us/aeronautics/skunkworks.html.

IT'S ABOUT TIME

"I DON'T HAVE THE TIME"

Have you said this in a meeting or a discussion with a colleague? Has this rolled off the tongue when confronted with an unexpected change, a new technology, or another initiative?

Many of us are stretched to our limits. A while ago, at a meeting of the Council of State Library Agencies in the Northeast in Cape May, New Jersey, I dined with librarians who were wearing many hats in their evolving institutions and working hard to meet the needs of the agencies they serve. I applaud the folks I meet like these who have absorbed more and more duties as staffing patterns have changed.

However, I bristle when I hear the "no time" response, because sometimes I think it's an excuse. It's a catchall phrase to sidestep learning something new, improving processes, or making a needed but oh-so-scary change. It leads me to ask a question in response: What do you actually make time for?

Do you clear your schedule for the pet project you just love? Do you personally handle every detail of your favorite task or responsibility, even when in the back of your mind you realize it might be done better, quicker, faster with some changes or streamlining? Do you hide out in your office or cubicle furtively reading gossip blogs when the rest of your department is off for development time or training?

TIME AFTER TIME

If you catch yourself at these avoidance activities, stop and consider the underlying reasons. It might be a trap you've fallen into and many folks you say it to are probably quick to back off or drop the discussion when you invoke the buzz of busyness. Sometimes we respond with "I don't have time" as an honest reflex and to elude the more difficult task of determining if there is something we should be giving up, or delegating, to make room for this new activity. Henry Ford once said, "Most people spend more time and energy going around problems than in trying to solve them."[1]

Other times, it may look like this: the library development staff works hard to bring a shiny new 23 Mobile Things learning program adaptation to your institution.[2] "I don't have time to participate," you say as a department manager. A possible translation: "I don't need to learn these things, I'm in management." The research I did on the impact of Learning 2.0 style programs found that staff members take cues from the participation or lack of participation by supervisors and administration.[3] It sets a definite tone if those in charge of the "learning organization" don't take time to learn themselves.

Moving a process online to save time sounds like a great idea, but it can become a daunting proposition if you don't feel your tech skills are up to snuff. "My time is very important to me" might translate to a confession that learning a new system is overwhelming, and that feels embarrassing. One of the best things we can do is own up to our need for time to learn, explore, and play with technologies that just might not be second nature to us. Put it out there and ask for help, but also offer your guidance and expertise to those who might be lacking in other areas where you excel.

CLOCK OF THE HEART

It may also be weariness, plain and simple. Let's call this "techno-fatigue," a close cousin to the infamous techno-stress. One more web form or one more thing to click on—and, yes, I actually heard someone say that in a meeting years ago—may be the last straw in a too-connected, too-techie workflow. Here, we might benefit from some of the mindfulness that comes with reflective practice.

Of course, we're not really talking about tech here; we're talking about how people respond to the demands of a constantly changing and evolving workplace.

Going forward, here's what I hope you'll make time for in your full and rich days: any opportunity to fine-tune skills, tech and otherwise; a chance to have a conversation with a mentor or mentee—we can learn from being both; or a frank discussion with your team about training needs, developing skills, and managing our most precious resource, time. What can we do differently? What delivers the most impact for the minutes and hours we spend? A person's priorities say more about him or her than most other things. Measure what you do. Look at the time you spend on every task during your day, during your staff's day. Where can you save?

Embrace constant change. "I have no time" is another way of saying, "I can't change; I'm too busy." Change allows growth, and without growth we will simply be running in circles.

One of my favorite songs reminds us that "time makes you bolder," and maybe that's a good thing to remember when someone requests a bit of your time.[4] Be bold and try that new process, new learning opportunity, or new idea. Another line from that same song? "I've been afraid of changing." Don't let that happen to you.

NOTES

1. Henry Ford, "Success," *The Forum,* October 1, 1928, 585, www.unz.org/Pub/Forum-19280ct-00583.
2. "About," 23 Mobile Things, http://23mobilethings.net/wpress/about/.
3. Michael Stephens, "Exemplary Practice for Learning 2.0: Based on a Cumulative Analysis for the Value and Effect of '23 Things' Programs in Libraries," *Reference and User Services Quarterly* 53, no. 2 (2013).
4. Stevie Nicks, Fleetwood Mac, "Landslide," record, Reprise Records, 1975.

THINGS THAT GO BUMP

WHAT KEEPS YOU UP AT NIGHT?

I ask this question at some of my library conference presentations as a way to break the ice and get people sharing. The answers are usually in a similar vein: budgets, e-books, and losing relevance. We might even call those answers the unholy trinity of librarian insomnia.

Relevance seems to be the most troublesome for our profession as we find ourselves yet again doing all those things that begin with "re": reimagining, reinvigorating, and renewing this, that, and the other. And just as librarians struggle with relevance, I sincerely hope that those of us in LIS education are doing the same. That keeps me up at night, especially when I hear from colleagues who question why they should be hiring LIS graduates when other skills and other degrees seem much more useful to the mission of the library.

CHECK UNDER THE BED

A few strategies with regard to relevance, then, to ease your sleep on a cold winter's night: get out there. Be visible. As reference statistics wane and paper reference collections dwindle, the need for a visible, vocal presence outside of our library walls is imperative. LIS schools that teach courses focused on marketing and advocacy are well positioned to produce grads that can get out into the community, make a case for increased or stable funding, and more. Pair those skills with a strong background in community building and technology, and it's a match made in heaven. Maybe the discussions (and apprehensions) surrounding the relevance of libraries and librarians are actually founded in our prevailing history of timidity and reticence.

Get serious about learning (of all kinds). One area of emphasis within the strategic mission of public libraries is lifelong learning, but all types of libraries can support this goal. Educator and researcher Roger Hiemstra argued that three forces propel a person's ongoing interest and need for lifelong learning: constant change, occupational obsolescence, and an individual's desire for self-actualization.[1] Libraries tap into these needs by providing learning opportunities, both formal (classes, lectures) and informal (at a desk, in the stacks, or out in the field).

Many people now turn to public libraries specifically for instruction and information on various technologies and applications. Providing training and assistance to patrons is a key area when offering technology-related services in public libraries. As technologies evolve, so does the need for more training opportunities.

A scan of the technology-related learning classes offered by some of the major public libraries in the United States also provides a snapshot of the need for tech-focused training. The popularity of classes concentrating on Internet resources, productivity applications such as those from Microsoft, and specialized classes on digital photography, online selling, and the various "hot" technologies of the day continues to expand.

The next step is more learning via various methods. Massive open online courses (MOOCs) for your patrons, anyone? The possibilities are endless. It makes sense, then, that LIS schools should ensure that students are versed in effective methods of teaching and promoting opportunities to learn in various ways.

Get creative. This doesn't have to involve 3-D printers. I am loving what I see happening in the "Idea Box" space of the Oak Park Public Library in Illinois.[2] Each month, a new creative activity is presented for patrons. Post-it notes sharing on the walls, learning opportunities, and arts and crafts all play a role: "Idea Box offers fresh ways to engage library customers in lifelong learning through creative play and fun."[3] Recently, the Idea Box offered a wall-sized Lite-Brite-type art project with colorful golf tees as the medium. Can you imagine the insights we might glean from user creations within projects like these?

PUT YOUR MIND AT EASE

This is doable in your library, folks. Look for ways to encourage the creativity of your users. Have some space to repurpose? Unleash ideas. Open minds. We are so much more than a book warehouse or Wi-Fi access point or a place that rents movies. Once we start believing it and acting on it, it'll be even easier for our users to do the same.

Meanwhile, LIS education needs to keep pace with these changes—from classes devoted to building and managing a creation/maker space to planning for services that push the limits of what a traditional library should be. Let's start preparing our students for tomorrow's libraries. When we've spent so much time teaching people how to collect and share items, it's a big step to teach people to create something new. Some folks say LIS students should take some classes outside of library school to get what they need. I'll continue to argue for a fluid, ever-evolving curriculum backed up by our core values. Rest up. Tomorrow looks great.

NOTES

1. Roger Hiemstra, *Lifelong Learning,* 3rd ed. (Fayetteville, NY: HiTree, 2002), http://roghiemstra.com/lllch1.html.
2. "Idea Box," Oak Park Public Library, http://oppl.org/events/idea-box.
3. Ibid.

EMBRACING CHAOS

IN *COGNITIVE SURPLUS,* Clay Shirky explores three ways that society might approach incorporating and adopting emerging technologies.[1] The scenarios include "traditionalist approval," "negotiated transition," and "as much chaos as we can stand." All could easily apply to how libraries, information centers, and educational institutions might respond to emerging technologies as well. Where does your organization fall?

TRADITIONAL ROADBLOCKS

Traditionalists want plans and services to move through the appropriate channels. Shirky uses the example of e-mail being placed under the control of the U.S. Postal Service.[2] That's like aligning a library's web presence with marketing and promotion. It may make sense, but participation from staff across the organization creates an even richer, human message in multiple voices. I learned long ago that library PR speak is just that—unless authenticity and transparency are guiding forces.

Sometimes, tradition collides with newer approaches that might make some uncomfortable. Several years ago, librarians shuttling me from the airport for a talk confided that most of their proposals had stopped on an administrator's desk. For weeks, nothing happened. That person had become a roadblock in every sense of the word. In my talk that day, I called for nimble action and for all to push their boundaries.

MEETING IN THE MIDDLE

In a "negotiated transaction," all stakeholders gather to iron out the best way to go forward. Radical ideas and "old school" methods meet at the same table to hash things out. I have an affinity for this approach. The traditionalists bring foundational thinking—what libraries have always done and what mission we serve—while the futurists cite current trends and evidence from recent studies to illustrate the need to incorporate new ideas such as a mobile site, tablet support, or gamification.

These groups, one hopes, meet in the middle to make something wonderful, but the opposite may occur, with greater friction when some participants fail to see the other's side. Negotiation and communication are key to "negotiated transition," as well as learning. The unknown can be scary, especially to traditionalists. Talking and exploring together is an antidote.

HERE COMES EVERYONE

Shirky, of course, advocates that we embrace "as much chaos as we can stand."[3] In this scenario, staff are encouraged to try out a new thing without regard to the way "it's always been done." This is messy, scary, and probably unwanted in most institutions. If the library can articulate the boundaries and define just how far out on the bleeding edge it will go with experimentation, that can set the stage for Shirky's ideal approach to emerging technologies.

In my early presentations with Jenny Levine about blogging and social participation within library services, folks expressed worry and even outrage that patrons might leave comments on library posts that were negative. This concern probably stopped a lot of library blogs outright or led to simple, one-way, comment-disabled broadcasting. Now, the ability to comment and participate seems to be built into everything—including checking in to your favorite TV show, reviewing hotels on TripAdvisor, sharing suggestions on Goodreads, and more. Control gives way to conversation. I recently heard a speaker call for "chaos in the catalog" as a means to involve everyone in creating the library's collection and access points. The audience bristled, but some applauded.

RESPONDING TO CHAOS

Part of me is tempted to argue that this is not a debate between those who want control and those who want chaos. The forward-thinking librarian understands that Shirky's "everybody's coming" is the future.[4] We are now living in the chaotic world, and we do not have a choice regarding where we can position ourselves. Our choice lies in how we respond. If we continue to respond to chaos using tools from the old world of control, then we will always fail. LIS students need to understand that the world is chaos, and it is our job to build our organizations in ways that can thrive within this chaos.

Calling for chaos implies a universe where it is impossible for an organization to respond and operate. This is not so. Control freaks like the word *chaos* because it gives them an out when it comes to operating in the current environment. By saying it's chaos they validate their slow, tedious, old-world management styles, even though such styles no longer work. Those unsigned proposals are a symptom of this mind-set.

We live in a world that multitasks—events and crises come concurrently, not singly or in a linear fashion. LIS management classes must teach future leaders to live and operate in that multitasking world. They must be able to juggle multiple crises and parallel events simultaneously. They must be flexible and nimble. They must be able to prioritize within that chaotic environment. Micromanagement does not work in a chaotic world. You'll never get anything done!

NOTES

1. Clay Shirky, *Cognitive Surplus: Creativity and Generosity in a Connected Age* (New York: Penguin, 2010).
2. Ibid., 209.
3. Ibid., 208.
4. Clay Shirky, *Here Comes Everybody: The Power of Organizing without Organizations* (New York: Penguin, 2008).

IN THE MOMENT

LIBRARIANS, ARE YOU present in your work? Are you listening when someone asks a question at the desk? LIS students, are you there in the classroom or online with an open mind and a thirst for learning? Are you in the moment?

My thoughts turn to mindfulness as I find many distractions pulling me away from grading, working on research, or reading student work. I want to be in the moment for all of these things. You've heard the advice: turn everything off to concentrate and get things done. But when so much of our personal and professional lives carry an online component, that can be hard to do. When writing, I usually shut down e-mail, instant messaging, and my browser, but then I hear the distant ding of the iPad in the other room. Some folks advocate having a technology-free zone in a certain room at home, but that's also a tough call when Wi-Fi pervades and devices move with us.

IS UNPLUGGING NECESSARY?

The popularity of "unplugging" continues to rise, but I was more interested in an article by Casey Cep, "The Pointlessness of Unplugging."[1] Cep explores the move to unplug as a means to reconnect with the "real" world, the authentic world. Cep argues that unplugging "suggests that the selves we are online aren't authentic, and that the relationships that we forge in digital spaces aren't meaningful. This is odd, because some of our closest friends and most significant professional connections are people we've only ever met on the Internet."[2] Imagine disconnecting from your personal learning networks or community of practice for longer than a weekend away or vacation time. You'd miss those colleagues, those friends. I know I would.

While adults struggle with unplugging and balance, more attention falls on young people. In my talks about "Learning Everywhere," I tell the story of young Ian, a neighbor who sometimes attaches to our Wi-Fi with his family's iPod Touch. "What are you doing, Ian?" I called out the window one day in summer. He held his device aloft and happily shouted, "I'm downloading apps." The world in which Ian will grow up will be a very different place.

More than once, someone in my audience has expressed concern that children and young people are always looking at their mobile device, texting, gaming, or whatever. Recently the comment was this: "I want to take away the iPad and send them outside. They are not in the moment." My reply was a reminiscence of my mother taking away my Hardy Boys books and sending me out to play one summer day. I was furious! The seminar room vibrated with comments: "It's the same thing." "It's not the same thing!"

WHY SOCIAL MATTERS

I'd argue that it is the same thing, with a slight caveat. In her new book, *It's Complicated: The Social Lives of Networked Teens,* Danah Boyd, a principal researcher at Microsoft Research, explores how young people use technology, pulling in findings from ten years of research.[3] I would suggest it should be required reading not only for parents and educators but also for librarians of all stripes. Boyd notes that "most teens are not compelled by gadgetry as such—they are compelled by friendship. The gadgets are interesting to them primarily as a means to a social end."[4]

Hangouts are now online as well as in real space. "What the drive-in was to teens in the 1950s and the mall in the 1980s," Boyd writes, "Facebook, texting, Twitter, instant messaging, and other social media are to teens now."[5] The caveat, then, is this: when taking away my books, the Hardy Boys would wait patiently for me, while unplugging a young person's potentially primary means of social interactivity could prove detrimental to their connections and friendships. Boyd shares the example of Heather, a teen who uses Facebook as "a social lifeline that enables her to stay connected to people she cares about but cannot otherwise interact with in person."[6] These young people are not sharing the same spaces, but they are sharing a moment.

Young people are doing what young people have always done. The tools are just a bit different. This is not an out, though, for a lack of conscientious parenting. Parents need to be involved as always. For educators and librarians, I'd argue that starting early with digital citizenship courses would serve young people well. I believe Boyd's work along with others such as *Hanging Out, Messing Around, and Geeking Out,* edited by Mizuko Ito, would support these initiatives.[7] In fact, isn't the popular YOUmedia space at the Chicago Public Library an extension of this: getting young people together to be social and learn with and around technology?[8]

So take a breath. We're okay. Our young people are okay. Technology is part of our lives. Unplugging is good, as is a balanced approach and an understanding of just how useful these devices and networks can be. Above all, no matter what the circumstance, be in the moment.

NOTES

1. Casey Cep, "The Pointlessness of Unplugging," *New Yorker,* March 19, 2014, www.newyorker.com/culture/culture-desk/the-pointlessness-of-unplugging.
2. Ibid.
3. Danah Boyd, *It's Complicated: The Social Lives of Networked Teens* (New Haven, CT: Yale University Press, 2014), www.danah.org/books/ItsComplicated.pdf.
4. Ibid., 18.
5. Ibid., 20.
6. Ibid.
7. Mizuko Ito, *Hanging Out, Messing Around, and Geeking Out: Kids Living and Learning with New Media* (Cambridge, MA: MIT Press, 2013).
8. YOUmedia, http://youmediachicago.org.

REFLECTIVE PRACTICE

AFTER THE SEMESTER ENDS

I often promise myself I will look for ways to be more mindful after a wonderful but exhausting semester. One thing I've done is return to yoga, the hot kind. In a recent morning class, the instructor ended by asking us to focus on the coming day. "What will you do with it?" she asked. "How will you be mindful today?" The turn of a calendar year is also a good time to remember reflective practice, whereby you take a moment, think about what you've learned, the experiences you've had in your workplace and career, and pull all of those things together as you encounter more choices. These processes are cyclical.

Reflective practice is mindfulness to the nth degree. It means being thoughtful about the decisions you make, about the projects you take on, and about how you put yourself out there in the online world. It might be what you present at a conference or what you write on a blog or in an article. Those things become part of your practice as well. It also means reflecting about the past. How did you come to be where you are in the field? What decisions did you make?

TRY TO BE VISIBLE

Amid our reflective practice, we need to remain visible. This is a fragile thing. It's something we have to work at all the time: our own practice and the collective practice of everyone who works in your particular environment, as well as our profession as a whole.

We must always keep working to be there, to be present, to be at the edge of what's happening, and to be very visible while focusing on people, not technology, not the collection. Those are merely tools. There is a wonderful quote I return to again and again: in *The Last Lecture,* Randy Pausch writes, "There is more than one way to measure profits and losses. On every level institutions can and should have a heart."[1]

PUTTING A FACE ON THE LIBRARY

This reminds me that the library should be human. It means that behind the keyboard, behind the blog, and behind the Facebook page, there's a person ready to have a conversation: ready to help, ready to listen.

For example, New Zealand's Christchurch City Libraries' Twitter page includes the photos of all of the official "tweeters" for the library.[2] I toured Christchurch recently. The city suffered in the earthquakes of 2010 and 2011. The libraries there adapted, sometimes changing locations, sometimes working in adverse conditions. Through it all, there has continued to be this strong Twitter presence that includes the human face of the library: those six smiling folks with their initials beside the thumbnail pics. They sign their tweets, in effect saying, "This is what I have to say. I'm representing the library, but this is me and this is my sort of human face on the library."

It pains me when I encounter librarians who refuse to share their photo online or wear a nametag while on duty. If we're seeking to build that human connection, that human relationship, it should start there. Stephen Abram said it best to me over dinner one night: "Would you go to doctors or seek out lawyers who refused to put their picture online?"

Lawrence Clark Powell wrote, "A good librarian is a librarian, a person with good health and warm heart, trained by study, and seasoned by experience to catalyze books and people."[3] That, my friends, is reflective practice. In 2014, I might paraphrase just a little differently: "Seasoned by experience to catalyze knowledge, information, and people."

INFINITE LEARNING

I've been talking a lot lately about the concept of infinite learning. I believe the library—all types of libraries—can be a focus, a hub for the potential for people always to learn. Think about how you might encourage people to learn and be curious, to show them how things work, and show them how to find their way.

I've often said that I believe librarianship is the ultimate service profession. As such, you may find yourself in a library job doing things that you did not anticipate you would do. It might be taking care of the restrooms when no one else is around, or getting someone to leave the building because they're being inappropriate. What we do is not simply what is written in our job descriptions. I've never known anyone who worked in a library who didn't, often, stray far and wide from the tasks they were hired to do. We cannot afford siloed mind-sets. We go where we are needed and do what is necessary to serve those who come to us. These are the things that we don't teach you in library school but do become part of your jobs, especially if you find your way into public service, being out there and being the face of the library.

NOTES

1. Randy Pausch and Jeffrey Zaslow, *The Last Lecture* (New York: Hyperion, 2008), 51.
2. "Christchurch City Libraries," Twitter, https://twitter.com/christchurchlib.
3. Lawrence Clark Powell, *The Little Package: Pages on Literature and Landscape from a Traveling Bookman's Life* (Cleveland, OH: World Publishing, 1964).

ACTIONS AND ANSWERS

I ONCE INVITED Char Booth, director of research, teaching, and learning services at the Claremont Colleges Library (and a 2008 *Library Journal* Mover & Shaker), to join my Hyperlinked Library class for an online social hour.[1] Our topic: reflective practice. Booth, author of *Reflective Teaching, Effective Learning: Instructional Literacy for Library Educators,* shared the work of John Dewey to highlight the attitudes required for reflective action in teaching.[2] Of course, the same can be applied to librarianship.

A CALL TO ACTION

The attitudes of reflective action, highlighted in an article by Grant and Zeichner (1984), include open-mindedness, responsibility, and wholeheartedness.[3] All are important and resonate deeply with me and my philosophy of what librarianship should be about. Approaching something with a sense of wholeheartedness means we are *all in* all the time, not just when it's convenient. It means bucking the status quo to do the right thing at the right moment. It means owning our actions as professionals.

I am most excited about this evolution of who we are and what we do on the ground and in the trenches. Folks meeting problems and challenges head-on every day via reflective action are the ones who will find solutions. Some of the projects and innovations we've seen recently add to a promising vision for the future.

REFRESHING IDEAS

A timely and moving example: Missouri's Ferguson Public Library staff rose to an incredible challenge and in my mind triumphed as they kept their doors open throughout the tumultuous times the city experienced in 2014.[4] The library became, in the words of the media and LIS folks, a safe place, an oasis, a refuge, and an inspiration. The donations that poured in via a library website PayPal link, hovering over $350,000, were indicative of what's possible even under the most dire circumstances.

Think of the challenges you've faced professionally. Budgets, personnel issues, technology, unruly users, and closed-minded governing bodies come to mind. How have you solved them? Or maybe it's the homeless, a test of service that many public libraries face every day, in towns large and small. A high degree of mindfulness—being open to new ideas and new ways of doing things—may be just the right fit.

Don't miss the *Library Journal* report highlighting the Edmonton Public Library's (EPL's) outreach program, which is being extended to five branches, that supports the city's homeless population.[5] Lisa Peet reported that in 2011, in response to the growing challenge of homeless people seeking shelter, "EPL became the first library in Canada to hire an outreach worker, Jared Tkachuk." When grant funding ran out, the library opted to continue the program. Read the piece. It's stirring.

The Salt Lake City Public Library (SLCPL) is exploring staying open 24 hours a day, 7 days a week.[6] This action seeks to make the library available to those who work during regular hours and can't make use of services and space. What a refreshing and interesting idea, which many libraries should consider if funding, staffing, and policy allow. I've met academic librarians who rave about their 24/7 initiatives, but this is my first encounter with an "open all night" public library. Sure, there's ongoing debate about who will be using the library at 3 A.M., but John Spears, SLCPL executive director, said "the regulations that apply to the library during the day are also on at night. We won't allow people to sleep or camp out."[7]

In another form of outreach that breaks down the barriers of the digital divide, I'm excited to read that the New York Public Library will be checking out Wi-Fi hot spots for free in a move to help the five boroughs provide access for all.[8] Finally, I'm reminded of what the Los Angeles Public Library is doing with the high school diploma program, filling a need in its community. The Career Online High School reaches citizens of Los Angeles via an online program that surely makes a difference in the lives of those who complete it.[9]

ANSWERS AHEAD

What might we take away from these ideas? I'd argue it's that the problems and challenges we face might be best answered through reflective action. These examples did not come about from hesitating, ignoring problems, or heaping on more restrictive policy but from meeting problems directly, not backing down, and moving ahead with our purpose firmly understood. I am hoping that we will see less professional self-questioning, less redefining of the profession, and more firm, outward-facing action performed with an open mind and heart.

NOTES
1. Char Booth, "Movers & Shakers 2008," *Library Journal*, http://lj.libraryjournal. com/2008/03/people/movers-shakers-2008/char-booth-movers-shakers-2008/#_.
2. Char Booth, *Reflective Teaching, Effective Learning: Instructional Literacy for Library Educators* (Chicago: American Library Association, 2011); John Dewey was a philosopher and psychologist in the late nineteenth and early twentieth centuries whose ideas impacted educational reform.
3. Carl A. Grant and Kenneth M. Zeichner, "On Becoming a Reflective Teacher," in *Preparing for Reflective Teaching* (Boston: Allyn & Bacon, 1984).
4. Lisa Peet, "Ferguson Library Provides Calm Refuge for a Torn Community," *Library Journal*, November 25, 2014, http://lj.libraryjournal.com/2014/11/ public-services/ferguson-library-provides-calm-refuge-for-a-torn-community/.
5. Lisa Peet, "Edmonton Public Library Adds Homeless Outreach to Five New Branches," *Library Journal*, December 4, 2014, http://lj.libraryjournal. com/2014/12/public-services/edmonton-public-library-adds-homeless-outreach-to-five-new-branches/.

6. Lisa Peet, "Salt Lake City Public Library Proposes 24/7 Operations," *Library Journal*, December 15, 2014, http://lj.libraryjournal.com/2014/12/library-services/salt-lake-city-public-library-proposes-247-operations/.
7. Ibid.
8. Matt Enis, "CPL, NYPL Wifi Hotspot Lending Programs Funded by Knight Foundation Grants," *Library Journal: The Digital Shift*, June 25, 2014, www.thedigitalshift.com/2014/06/digital-divide/cpl-nypl-wifi-hotspot-lending-programs-funded-knight-foundation-grants/.
9. Ian Chant, "Gale, Libraries Team to Offer High School Diplomas," *Library Journal*, January 9, 2014, http://lj.libraryjournal.com/2014/01/public-services/gale-libraries-team-to-offer-high-school-diplomas/.

WHAT'S YOUR PITCH?

SPEAKING HERE AND there, I've logged a few airline miles over the years and visited some pretty cool places. A short while ago, I was coming back from the New York Library Association conference, flying from Albany to Chicago, and I was seated next to a friendly young man who asked me what I did for a living.

This can sometimes be an awkward conversation. It can go any number of ways. "I'm a professor" is one answer. "I teach," another. When I say "libraries," sometimes my seatmate's eyes glaze over, and I get the typical, "Aren't libraries going away?" question or a joke about the Dewey Decimal System or some other very telling response that makes it easy to see exactly how that person feels about libraries.

This fellow perked right up. It turns out my neighbor, Colin Ryan, was a comedian and motivational speaker who had recently done a program at New York's Saratoga Springs Library. He had many positive things to say about Director A. Isaac Pulver's staff and the audience. He was thrilled with the crowd that had packed the meeting room to laugh at and learn from his talk on managing money. He also had some interesting and well-thought-out questions for me about libraries. No eye-glazing, no invocations of "Won't Google save us all?"

AIRPLANES AND ELEVATORS

Our conversation got me thinking about my airplane pitch, also known as the elevator speech. It's the answer you give to the "What do you do?" question. My patter has changed over the years, from talking about my public library work to the "in the elevator at an Association for Library and Information Science Education conference and looking for a teaching position" line describing my research agenda and educational philosophy.

Google "elevator pitch" and you'll find plenty of "how-to" sites, mainly aimed at helping business folks sell their products. Tips include rephrasing "I'm in sales" to "I sell mobile solutions that help businesses maximize profits." You'll also find suggestions for selling yourself as a job seeker, another role of the pitch. It's a good exercise for information professionals to consider what their elevator spiel might be. Here are a few of the various ways we might use a well-deliberated pitch.

ADVOCATING FOR YOUR LIBRARY

I recall being in line at the movies back in the 1990s. "Hey, you're the 'AV Guy,'" said someone nearby, referencing my then position and department at the St. Joseph County Public Library (SJCPL) in South Bend, Indiana. "That's me," I said. This led to a chat about what the SJCPL offered in music and movies. Looking back, I could have said so much more.

Now, it's a given that we should be prepared to tell folks who recognize us from our places of employment just what the library can do for the community. Not interested in chatting outside the confines of your library about the benefits your institution provides? It might be time to reassess your attitude. This is a call to action for all staff to become evangelists for the library.

ADVOCATING FOR ALL LIBRARIES

This is a good one for the airplane or while traveling. Not only are we advocates for our own institutions, we're also advocates for the profession and the mission of libraries in general. How do you describe what I've called the "ultimate service profession"? It's easy to fall into some of the clichés the media uses—we're not "shushing" anymore—but focusing on both the foundational tenets and the evolving nature of our profession might be a better route. This might be a good exercise to do with colleagues or your staff as well as a fun experiment for your students: brainstorm the broadest of library-focused elevator speeches.

ADVOCATING FOR YOURSELF

This might be during the job search or if you are seeking to move up in your institution or the profession. In a time when shameless self-promotion is often painfully obvious in many online channels, talking about yourself, the work you do, and what it means to you is an art. Be humble but authentic. Share your passions, successes, and failures.

PITCHING YOURSELF

All of these approaches require a high degree of reflection. They are also about defining how we view ourselves. Making our elevator speeches good and solid will help us define our roles and what we hope to achieve. Elevator speeches should be as much about what we've done as what we plan to do.

Many of us go through periods in which we're not sure what "good" we're doing and what role we and the library are playing. Perfecting this patter means we have to figure out some of these things, which often helps us redefine our goals and redirect our efforts.

What's your elevator pitch? What statements have you used to educate and advocate for the library? Which worked the best, and what have you changed over time?

COLOR ME CURIOUS

IT STARTS *WITH* US

I use that phrase on a slide in my talks and course lectures and whenever I get the chance to talk about librarians, libraries, and our continual adaptation to societal and technological change. It's also closely related to my thoughts on professional development and learning in the workplace. This isn't sweeping organizational change; this time it's personal.

No amount of training or professional development can move us forward if an individual is uninterested in learning or growing. I'd argue for two vital traits that will serve librarians well throughout their careers. Longtime librarians, mid-career folks, new hires, and students, I'm talking to you! The traits are simple yet pack a powerful punch: curiosity and creativity.

NURTURING YOUR CURIOSITY

Curiosity about the world and how people create, use, and access information should fuel our practice. It should also drive ongoing evaluation of services and user needs. When a librarian asks me how to figure out what new services, tech, or materials to provide, I'll always start with "ask your users." In *A Curious Mind: The Secret to a Bigger Life*, authors Brian Grazer and Charles Fishman promote curiosity conversations, or discussions with accomplished strangers, that led Grazer to develop some notable television shows and movies.[1] For us, it might be similar chats with constituents, colleagues, and those who inspire us. How interesting might it be to sit down with city commissioners, the provost, the school superintendent, or the CEO and speak with them about their perceptions of what libraries do?

MAINTAINING YOUR CREATIVITY

Acting on what our curiosity reveals might lead to some innovative approaches to service. Maybe users have told you they visit the library to browse and serendipitously discover something new. "Out of the box" displays of materials and spaces devoted to learning new things, such as the classes taught with sewing machines and 3-D printers at the White Plains Public Library in New York, can spark creativity in ourselves and our users.[2] And the emerging trend of adult coloring books? Johanna Basford's *Secret Garden* coloring book is a hit among adults, and the idea is expanding (e.g., a *Game of Thrones*-inspired book).[3] NPR recently ran a story by Barbara J. King, who highlighted her own experience coloring as she dealt with the passing of her mother: "Coloring brings a different kind of sensual engagement, one that perhaps echoes the embodied pleasures found in creative cooking, gardening, and carpentry."[4] In coloring, King also notes she found a comfort steeped in memories of childhood. The article prompted Stacie Ledden at Colorado's Anythink Libraries to ponder on Facebook, "What if a library set up a coloring station in a busy part of their community to offer a little artistic reprieve in people's days? Maybe at bus stops, at the mall, the DMV, the park?" That is creative thinking in action!

THE ZERO SUM LIBRARIAN

The techniques above might balance some of the discourse we fall back on that could be construed as zero sum thinking. We could never launch twenty-three mobile things during summer reading months, right? Staff are just too busy! We can't launch new maker initiatives because we are still teaching people to use a mouse, right? What if the sewing machine breaks?

Maybe that learning course for staff timed with summer reading will offer some insight into new directions such a tried-and-true program might take. Mouse skills may eventually no longer be needed, but as long as they are, we can help. That doesn't mean we shouldn't also be looking forward and talking with key players about what other learning opportunities the library might offer. How wonderful would it be to find a YouTube video detailing a simple repair to a sewing machine and learn how to do it with your users? I bounced these ideas off of John Blyberg, assistant director at Darien Library, Connecticut, and a 2006 *Library Journal* Mover & Shaker.[5]

He commented, "You don't need to know how to use a mouse in order to have curiosity, you just need to love the world and want to be engaged with it." Amen.

I may not always agree with the comparison of librarianship to other professions, but in professional development the examples are many: doctors, lawyers, auto mechanics, airline pilots, and so on. All of them must learn, on a regular basis, about changes to the tools and processes of their field. To fight growth, to rebuke learning, is the same as not updating that annual edition reference book, or not inserting the revised legal codes into the law book. No excuses.

The willingness, the desire, the need to learn and grow is what defines librarians and librarianship. Following the creative spark, nurtured by curiosity, to where it leads us may yield surprising results.

NOTES

1. Brian Grazer and Charles Fishman, *A Curious Mind: The Secret to a Bigger Life* (New York: Simon & Schuster, 2015).
2. White Plains Public Library, http://whiteplainslibrary.org/category/classes/.
3. Johanna Basford, *Secret Garden: An Inky Treasure Hunt and Coloring Book* (London: Laurence King, 2013); George R. R. Martin, *The Official A Game of Thrones Coloring Book: A Song of Ice and Fire* (New York: Bantam Books, 2015).
4. Barbara J. King, "For Adults, Coloring Invites Creativity and Brings Comfort," *NPR 13.7 Cosmos & Culture: Commentary on Science and Society,* June 11, 2015, www.npr.org/sections/13.7/2015/06/11/413603343/for-adults-coloring-invites-creativity-and-brings-comfort.
5. John Blyberg, "Movers & Shakers 2006," *Library Journal,* http://lj.libraryjournal.com/2006/03/people/movers-shakers-2006/john-blyberg-movers-shakers-2006/.

2

SCANNING THE HORIZON

*Challenges, Developments,
Emerging Opportunities*

I
T'S AN EASY formula but daunting nonetheless. Scanning the
horizon plus talking to users equals a bright future for our field.
Various reports, executive summaries, futurist presentations, and
user research contribute to our view of where libraries are headed.
These are tools that allow us to focus on the future we are building
for our constituents. We must capitalize on these opportunities to
use everything at our disposal—technology, our buildings, evolving
services—to reach all users wherever and whenever they need us.

The user is the center of this expanding universe of access and
information. Utilizing user-focused research and *talking* to our constituents—beyond just a web survey and chatting with people who
come through our doors—ensures we are on the right track. Let's
leave a good impression so that our users come back to us in-person
and online.

It seems sometimes that not a week goes by without a major article in the press either touting some new, cool, out-of-the-ordinary
thing libraries are doing or a doom and gloom scenario that libraries will soon go the way of drive-up photo developing booths! What
lies ahead for librarians? The general public may ooh and ahh at
these stereotypical pieces but we know better. Librarians who evolve
along with technology and look forward to new ideas and changing
environments will be the "full stack" employees who enliven their

coworkers and patrons with a realistic vision of what comes next. The ability to learn about and adapt services to emerging technologies will always be a given. We should start practicing this during graduate education in our field.

SCANNING THE HORIZON

IF YOU ARE on the fence about emerging technologies, take a look at the *Horizon Report.*[1] Over the years, these reports not only present technologies to watch but offer a road map for planning and an ongoing dialogue about change in education, learning, and libraries. Supported by research and evidence, it points the way to the future. This rich trove will spark your thinking, as it always does mine. Here are some of my observations and ideas on the 2011 report.

CONVERSATION-BASED READING

Reading becomes social. While the e-book market continues to steamroll past libraries, the 2011 report offers an intriguing concept: "What makes electronic books a potentially transformative technology is the new kinds of reading experiences that they make possible."[2] Reading can remain a solitary, enjoyable activity for all, but some may choose to experience a more conversation-based form of consumption of content.

I've long included "context books" in my teaching—notable titles centered on social issues, learning, and technology outside our field to illustrate LIS concepts and expand students' purview. One semester, I used the highlighting feature on my Kindle to clip passages in Peter Morville's *Ambient Findability* and Nick Bilton's *I Live in the Future.*[3] Those thought-provoking bits sit on a web page devoted to my reading. I can choose to tweet those highlights and 140-character commentaries to my classes via a hashtag. I can display highlights and commentary of selected context books within my course sites. In turn, students will be able to comment on the passages, as well as retweet them to others.

The Kindle's new Public Notes feature further expands the possibilities by incorporating annotations from everyone who opts in: authors, commentators, fans, and so on. Group reading/thinking/ tweeting/sharing will come next, with streams of insights flowing from various devices into a larger conversation. Eventually we may see LIS classes engaging directly with authors, other students, practicing librarians, and scholars to discuss and debate a work via these new channels for reading.

EXPANDING READERS' ADVISORY

I once had a lively class discussion about a "what if" scenario: what if social reading was combined with augmented reality (AR), another emerging technology the report identifies? AR adds a layer of digital information "over the real world, creating a reality that is enhanced."[4] When all you see on the subway, bus, or in the café is a nondescript e-reader, the traditional conversation-starter, commenting on someone's book, hits a snag. But what if the devices could someday create a zone where the current title on one reader displays on someone else's device (e.g., "Three people in this café are also reading *The Girl Who Kicked the Hornet's Nest*") or floats above readers' heads when viewed through a smartphone app? Imagine the possibilities for readers' advisory in this world.

Social reading offers all sorts of potential for libraries. Couldn't we organize these kinds of reading groups as well, possibly aggregating highlights and comments into a virtual readers' community? Imagine a portion of the library's web presence devoted to gathering and sharing e-book highlights, comments, and discussion among group members, library staff, and authors. Of course, the site would be optimized for the device of the user's choice.

UPENDING EDUCATION

Social reading and the other technologies identified have potential for education. New models and new delivery methods are already trumping the status quo. Learning does not have to wait until everyone is assembled in a classroom at an appointed day and hour. The lines between face-to-face classes and online courses are beginning to blur. Students will carry their course content with them on tablets and mobiles. Creativity in learning objects and media of all kinds will usurp mind-numbing lectures. View the University of Bergen's takeoff on Dickens, "A Plagiarism Carol," which teaches students about academic integrity through an entertaining video story.[5] The best avenues for learning remain discussion and exploration facilitated by a guiding professor, working with such new technologies.

Imagine an interactive Flipboard-style tablet app that affords professors and students the chance to craft their own textbooks related to a course from websites, open access articles, and social sites. I'd much rather have my research articles there for active comment and expansion than mired in the peer-review process and copyright. Imagine how we might teach the reference interview or an introduction to classification via a game-based system. Imagine student projects focused on creating AR environments for information sharing and exchange. The first steps might be basic apps that offer location-based help throughout the library or the community itself. The next would be info-rich digital space anchored to geographic location curated by librarians and created by users.

Explore the *Horizon Reports* for yourself. What can you imagine?

NOTES

1. *Horizon Report*, www.nmc.org/nmc-horizon/.
2. Larry Johnson, Rachel Smith, H. Willis, Alan Levine, and K. Haywood, *The 2011 Horizon Report* (Austin, TX: New Media Consortium, 2011), 8, www.nmc.org/sites/default/files/pubs/1316814265/2011-Horizon-Report(2).pdf.
3. Peter Morville, *Ambient Findability: What We Find Changes Who We Become* (Sebastopol, CA: O'Reilly Media, 2005); Nick Bilton, *I Live in the Future and Here's How It Works: Why Your World, Work, and Brain Are Being Creatively Disrupted* (New York: Crown Business, 2011).
4. Johnson, Smith, Willis, Levine, and Haywood, *The 2011 Horizon Report*, 16, www.nmc.org/sites/default/files/pubs/1316814265/2011-Horizon-Report(2).pdf.
5. YouTube, https://www.youtube.com/watch?v=Mwbw9KF-ACY.

REACHING ALL USERS

A RECENT STUDY by the Pew Internet & American Life Project, "How Americans Value Public Libraries in Their Communities," included this finding: "Some 90 percent of Americans ages 16 and older said that the closing of their local public library would have an impact on their community, with 63 percent saying it would have a 'major' impact."[1] What's intriguing is that only 29 percent reported that it would have a major impact on the respondent and respondent's family. In other words, 90 percent of folks do not want the library to close, but many fewer would feel the negative consequences.

REACHING OUT

This reminds me of some questions that have dogged librarians since we first opened our doors. Are we reaching everyone we can? Are we giving them services they want to use? Are we giving them a reason to depend upon us?

As a professor, one unit I enjoy teaching is called "Reaching All Users." I appreciate it because I can surprise my students with a bit of a bait and switch. Reaching everyone means using technology to offer new ways to interact with the library, yes, but it also encompasses a wide array of channels for interaction across virtual and physical planes. And one of the things that we always need to keep thinking about is how we can connect with our users, find ways to be present in their lives, and let them know what we can do for them. What little things can we do? And how about some big ideas and big thinking?

Here in Michigan, Ann Arbor District Library Assistant Director Eli Neiberger reported that the library shook things up by deciding that summer at the library wasn't just for kids nor just for readers. His purpose? To unlock an enthusiastic new audience for the district. My home library, which was in Traverse City, launched Books & Brewskis, a book discussion sponsored by the library and held in a local microbrewery. And Jen Waller, a librarian at Miami

University in Oxford, Ohio, told me that we must use "multi-pronged approaches to reach all users! One of the ways we strive to do it: we're open 24/7," with circulation staff available at all hours of the night.

On the virtual side, I appreciated a past job listing at the Skokie Public Library in Illinois for a virtual community engagement manager. Anticipated duties included managing the online presence for the library and consulting with the community engagement manager and other administrators to use virtual services to further the overall strategic plan of the library. Take a look at British Columbia's Vancouver Public Library's "Connect with VPL" page to see examples of all the virtual streams that folks can explore.[2] Seeing library patrons Ann and Teresa highlighted in a photo on the library's front page with the caption "We love mobile services from the library" brings the physical and virtual together.[3]

LIS TO LEADERSHIP

Years ago, I spent an evening at an American Library Association (ALA) Annual Conference dining with the folks from Darien Library, Connecticut. Seated next to Louise Berry, Darien's director (who later retired), I marveled at her ideas for involving all levels of staff in library decision-making and user-focused collection development. I had to ask Louise, "What should I be teaching in library school? What should our LIS students come to you prepared to do?"

"Be leaders," she said. "Be innovators. They should be the ones watching and planning for the future."

That charge resonated. Leaders, yes. Doing time in an entry-level library job waiting for someone to retire or leave for the chance to move up, no. Put smart-minded, tech-savvy folks of all backgrounds at service points and free up your trained professionals for higher-level duties and strategizing on ways to meet needs.

It starts with some questions. Whom do you reach well? Who uses your library passionately? Take care of them and keep them. Who doesn't use the library? Who in your community could benefit from access, services, assistance? Find them. Go to them, ask them what they want and need.

How can we respond to those requests? How can we let them know what we're doing? It's a multistep process related to being transparent. It includes listening very closely to what your users are saying, even if you don't like it, even if it pushes the boundaries of what you think the library should be. You might listen in focus groups or surveys or online in social networks. It might mean performing a community analysis on a granular neighborhood, campus, or department level. Also, listen to what people are not saying. If the tech-savvy, for example, no longer use your spaces or ask you questions, for example, then perhaps you're not meeting their needs.

Certainly, one important theme is finding balance for our services and projects. Cultivating thriving virtual learning communities with broad, beyond-the-walls outreach managed by future-thinking professionals seems like the way forward to reaching as many users as possible.

NOTES

1. Kathryn Zickuhr, Lee Rainie, Kristen Purcell, and Maeve Duggan, "How Americans Value Public Libraries in Their Communities," Pew Research Center's Internet & American Life Project, December 11, 2013, http://libraries.pewinternet.org/files/legacy-pdf/PIP_Libraries%20in%20communities.pdf, 1.
2. "Connect with VPL," Vancouver Public Library, www.vpl.ca/about/generic/connect.
3. Vancouver Public Library, www.vpl.ca/.

MOBILE AT THE LIBRARY

I REMEMBER UNPACKING (slowly, slowly) my new iPhone 5S in a major moment of personal technolust. I was upgrading from a quickly aging iPhone 4 and the larger screen size, fingerprint identification, and enhanced camera pulled me in. It also caused me to reflect on the mobile device and its touchstone role with people in general and librarians in particular. What a history we've had together!

BEWARE THE FUTURE

Sharing images of library signs—especially those related to mobile devices and their use within library buildings—was part of my early focus on how libraries interact with their users via signage.[1] Aaron Schmidt, writing *Library Journal*'s "User Experience" column, has also explored these ideas, especially in "Signs of Good Design."[2] Language usually attached to an image of a mobile phone with the red circle and line through it was of this variety: "Violators will be asked to leave," "Conversations not allowed," and one was signed ominously by "the Library Director." Other signage you may have seen passed around Buzzfeed and LIS blogs warn that food or drink near library computers would bring "the wrath of the library director." When did the position of director become so scary? When did we become so mean?

I poked a bit of fun at these signs at the expense of the library that posted them and was called out more than once. But for every bad sign that went up, I believe many more came down, as librarians took to making kindness audits of signage and spaces. "Quiet conversation, please," and "Don't forget to set your phone to vibrate," are much more user-positive admonitions.

A WORLD OF INFORMATION

Years ago, I did a presentation for a group of librarians, LIS faculty, and students in South Carolina. The night before the talk, the hotel bartender chatted with me about his mobile device. He was playing the bar's music from his iPhone. We started talking about apps we liked and the ways we used our phones, and he said, "I have everything I need here: I have my web, I have my e-mail, I have my text, I have my video, and I have my music: *I have the world of information in my hand.*" His remark resonated with me, and I have told the story in many presentations since, because it's indicative of the way that people think about their devices. This is supported by recent research that might just surprise you.

IT'S ALL ABOUT TIME

A joint study by AOL Inc. and the advertising firm Batten, Barton, Durstine, and Osborn recently revealed that "68 percent of consumer mobile phone use occurs in the home" and indicated that folks have seven primary motivations for using mobile devices.[3] The descriptors included self-expression, discovery, preparation (planning a trip, etc.), and accomplishment of a task (mobile banking, etc.). The highest use, however, at 46 percent, is what the researchers called "me time," defined as "seeking relaxation and entertainment in order to indulge oneself or pass the time." The study, aimed at marketers, should also inspire us—librarians—to seek ways "to help users indulge and enjoy themselves."

Pew's "Cell Phone Activities"[4] and "Cell Internet Use" reports from fall 2013 provide further evidence that our mobile devices are ingrained in our lives.[5] The latter report notes that younger adults and those with lower income and education are more likely to use their cell phones as their primary method for accessing the Internet.[6] This is important information for companies, organizations, and libraries to consider when trying to reach these groups.

IT'S ALL ABOUT THEM

The North Carolina State University James B. Hunt Library's Instagram contest is an example of turning "me time" into a collaborative, participatory project for students. Invited to shoot artistic and fun images of the new Hunt, students' snaps, tagged #huntlibrary, were displayed around the space and online. The students, armed with their smartphones, created a unique library collection.[7]

The day after receiving my new phone, I traveled to Missouri to make a presentation. During free time, I visited a local county library branch, happening upon a librarian roaming the stacks with an iPad. She approached me and inquired if I needed help. No, I said, but I was very interested in how the iPad was working for her as a reference device. She had positive views, talking about how the library was working to use technology more effectively to interact with patrons. She was optimistic about the future of the service. We parted, and I walked from the stacks to the main reference area, where I was greeted by a sign: "Cell phone use is prohibited." Posting a shot of it to Instagram, I tagged it to my classes: "There's still work to be done."

NOTES

1. Tame the Web, http://tametheweb.com/category/signage-in-libraries/.
2. Aaron Schmidt, "Signs of Good Design," *Library Journal: The User Experience,* February, 1, 2011, http://lj.libraryjournal.com/2011/02/opinion/aaron-schmidt/signs-of-good-design-the-user-experience/#_.
3. "Joint Study from AOL and BBDO Turns Traditional View of Mobile Space on Its Head," *PR Newswire,* October 3, 2012, www.prnewswire.com/news-releases/joint-study-from-aol-and-bbdo-turns-traditional-view-of-mobile-space-on-its-head-172448781.html.
4. Maeve Duggan, "Cell Phone Activities 2013," Pew Research Center's Internet & American Life Project, September 16, 2013, www.pewinternet.org/2013/09/19/cell-phone-activities-2013/.
5. Maeve Duggan and Aaron Smith, "Cell Internet Use 2013," Pew Research Center's Internet & American Life Project, September 16, 2013, www.pewinternet.org/2013/09/16/cell-internet-use-2013/.
6. Ibid., 2.
7. Jason Casden, Mike Nutt, Cory Lown, and Bret Davidson, "My #HuntLibrary: Using Instagram to Crowdsource the Story of a New Library," *ACRL Tech Connect,* May 13, 2013, http://acrl.ala.org/techconnect/post/my-huntlibrary-using-instagram-to-crowdsource-the-story-of-a-new-library; Matt Enis, "NCSU Shares Open-Source Solution for Crowdsourcing Photos," *Library Journal: The Digital Shift,* August 16, 2013, www.thedigitalshift.com/2013/08/social-media/ncsu-shares-open-source-solution-for-crowdsourcing-photos/; Meredith Schwartz, "Tomorrow, Visualized," *Library Journal: Library by Design,* September 18, 2013, http://lj.libraryjournal.com/2013/09/buildings/lbd/tomorrow-visualized-library-by-design-fall-2013/#_.

STACKING THE DECK

HAVE YOU READ ABOUT THE "FULL STACK EMPLOYEE"?

In a think piece published in *Medium*, author Chris Messina—the creator of the hashtag, no less—offers this definition: "the full stack employee has a powerful combination of skills that make them incredibly valuable. They are adept at navigating the rapidly evolving and shifting technological landscape. They make intuitive decisions amidst information-abundance, where sparse facts mingle loosely with data-drenched opinions."[1] It's a tech-heavy take, but bear with me, as Messina broadens the definition: "Full stack employees have an insatiable appetite for new ideas, best practices, and ways to be more productive and happy. They're curious about the world, what makes it work, and how to make their mark on it."

Maybe you've interviewed these types or hired them. Maybe you've watched a longtime employee evolve into a full stack powerhouse. If you haven't encountered them, I argue you soon will, especially as new grads in tech-oriented library and information programs come looking for positions. As buzz-wordy as this pancake-invoking moniker seems to be, I believe the description merits some consideration as we examine our evolving workforce.

ALWAYS ON

Full stacks know how to self-promote "tastefully," says Messina, going beyond the rock star-type, all-show-and-no-content, to engage and share with their audience.[2] I'd argue that library-type full stacks are those folks we see working hard at their jobs, sharing their successes and failures in Twitter chats and in other social streams, and seeking to make a mark that has meaning within the profession. They're not the ones preening and posing at conferences or proclaiming that the next big thing is XYZ because they said so.

These folks are seemingly always on and always connected. This is both a good and a bad thing, Messina notes.[3] Balance, as usual in all things, is a goal. Maybe the full stacks have a flavor of mindfulness that many of us have yet to find as we move among channels, messages, and queries. Or maybe this is the failure of the "rebranding of the perfect tech employee," as Elea Chang points out in a counterpoint post.[4] Messina, however, sees a constantly moving scale: "Being full stack is an exercise in shifting between opposite poles."[5]

MAKING ROOM FOR FULL STACKS

One challenge is how libraries can accommodate these eager employees. A library director I spoke with about these folks said, "I have a few. They're the young ones. Let them succeed. They are *so* different from other employees who think they are goofing off much of the time." John Szabo, city librarian, Los Angeles Public Library, told me, "They are also well connected to their peers, involved in formal and informal professional groups, and share a deep passion for the public library mission."

We might begin to explore how co-working spaces could look like in our institutions. How might the "reference workroom" become more like those spaces born out of the tech world in which disparate groups work together? What if your employees had a number of spaces to work "off desk" and mix and mingle? Maybe mixing everyone up will lead to some intriguing and fruitful partnerships between the full stacks and other staff.

Consider alternative schedules that support the services of the library but maybe with a bit more flexibility for the "always on." This is a difficult hurdle for public institutions: working anywhere, anytime doesn't fit well with the time card-punching, management-ruled world of work. As Messina notes, "Just because they demand a high degree of flexibility and autonomy doesn't mean that they get to dictate the criteria by which their work is evaluated. That's still the role of the manager."[6]

I recognize this trait in my students. They are inspired, engaged, and usually go way beyond the requirements of assignments, because they care. LIS programs should nurture the development of full stacks in LIS programs in similar ways as will be done by the libraries that hire them. I'd venture that cutting-edge classes and strong foundational curricula would entice full stackers to excel.

NO GENERALISTS

While Messina defines full stacks as polymaths, I disagree.[7] Full stacks don't present themselves as masters of every subject out there. We know that's not possible, nor do we subscribe to that mind-set in our profession. Full stacks are different. They are conduits, connectors, discoverers. They are the people you want to let loose in your community, the ones you want to embed in community or campus organizations.

Watch for the full stacks. Maybe some will come to you with backgrounds in tech and newly minted MLIS degrees, forgoing the start-up lifestyle for a focus on people and improving services to them. Welcome the full stacks into the mix. And note that Messina argues for a high degree of empathy "both for this new kind of employee, but also from them."[8] That's something we can surely agree is beneficial to our mission.

NOTES

1. Chris Messina, "The Full-Stack Employee," *Medium,* April 7, 2015, https://medium.com/@chrismessina/the-full-stack-employee-ed0db089f0a1#.d0wffctcb.
2. Ibid.
3. Ibid.
4. Elea Chang, "The Full-Stack Employee and the Glorification of Generalization," *Modern View Culture: Technology, Culture and Diversity Media,* April 15, 2015, https://modelviewculture.com/news/the-full-stack-employee-and-the-glorification-of-generalization.
5. Messina, "The Full-Stack Employee," https://medium.com/@chrismessina/the-full-stack-employee-ed0db089f0a1#.d0wffctcb.
6. Ibid.
7. Ibid.
8. Ibid.

3

CONSIDERATIONS FOR PROSPECTIVE LIBRARIANS

POTENTIAL LIBRARIANS SHOULD realize that information professions require an online presence and the desire to be engaged in online conversation with users and colleagues. This is the scenario of the future. In fact, future librarians should ask themselves why they are entering this profession. They may need to look beyond the trite "I like books" to more complex answers like "I want to reach users beyond the physical library space using emerging technologies."

Another key question for individuals contemplating a master's in library science (MLS) is what program they want. Many factors must be weighed: currency of curriculum, delivery of courses face-to-face or online, and so on.

More and more, online options are available for MLS programs. This change brings up concerns about accreditation and quality, but the future looks positive. So many technological opportunities are available to make online teaching and learning engaging, thought-provoking, and skill-enhancing. The best online programs are those that deliver human engagement and collaboration, as geographical barriers and time zones fall away.

Students going through MLS programs need to start developing an attitude of professionalism now as they interact with fellow students and professors and as they meet colleagues in libraries and at conferences. Now is the time to engage in professional conversations in-person and online, all the while remembering that the quality of the message trumps the reach of it.

All librarians—the students-in-training, the beginning professionals, and the veterans—should seek out challenges and should ever be learning.

IS LIBRARIANSHIP FOR YOU?

IN MY TEACHING and research, I am always exploring what's happening in LIS education. I regularly read and engage in the ongoing discourse about LIS schools. I discuss research that informs us, our users, and our facilities, and stories from the trenches on the realities of working toward a degree at a time when libraries are facing serious competition. Google, Netflix, Apple, Amazon, and the Web itself are all in the running for bits and pieces of our core services and foundational practices. Just as librarians work to align with our fast-changing world, so should LIS education.

USING THE PAST AS PROLOGUE

I finished my MLS in 1995. I had very little contact beyond the classroom with my instructors at Indiana University South Bend (IU's Bloomington-based program had spread across many of the satellite campuses). One instructor drove two hours each way from Chicago to teach once a week. Another was the busy director of a local public library. In those days before ubiquitous e-mail, it seemed very difficult to have contact with instructors outside of class meeting nights. Feedback, updates, and announcements were delivered in class, via written comments on my assignments, and only occasionally by telephone.

Jump ahead nearly a decade. In 2003 I discovered the perfect combination of an Apple laptop, free Wi-Fi at Panera Bread (think food café), and the wonders of blog publishing. Panera became my "mobile office," and many mornings I stopped there before heading to the St. Joseph County Public Library in South Bend, Indiana, for my job as head of tech training and web development. I would read RSS feeds of other bibliobloggers, write a post or two, and explore what was happening on the Web. These were my own professional development "office hours." I can't count how many times I took a citation or a blog post URL I'd found to a meeting at SJCPL to share with other staff as we worked on projects.

WE'RE ALL MOBILE

A few years later, teaching at Dominican University in River Forest, Illinois, my classroom was filled with students who brought their own laptops and other mobile devices. We stayed in touch via course websites running WordPress and BuddyPress (a social suite of plugins). Just recently, I taught remotely during a five-week research tour of Australia. For another class, I recorded video updates for my students as I hiked in northern Michigan. My "office" and the opportunities to connect with my students are unlimited.

The best thing about all of these technological advances is that LIS students have access to practitioners and professionals all over the world if they choose to participate. My students don't have a choice: I expect them to join in the online world, beyond the closed systems used in many online classes. In fact, my syllabi state, "This is also a way for students to experience the emerging social nature of the web—similar systems are being used in library settings all over the world. Librarians are working, writing, and sharing in open, online systems created for interaction with each other and with library users." I do allow students to use a pseudonym or avatar if they prefer not to use their full name or photo online.

If you are a current LIS student and have not spent some time inside these online environments, do it as soon as possible. If you are a future LIS student looking for a program, examine the technology offerings of your potential schools very closely. Every aspect of what librarians do—from collection development, information services, and web presence to story time, circulation, and programming—is or will be touched in some way by technology.

JOIN THE CONVERSATION

If the online world is not for you, then neither may be a career in librarianship. The most prevalent LIS jobs in the next few years will probably be ones where you're not tied to your desk and you communicate well beyond the physical walls of the building.

It's not just students who should participate in this online world. Librarians must find their niche as well. Over five years ago the conversation went on in blogs. Now it flows vibrantly across media platforms, enabling a stronger connection with library users through marketing, outreach, and the human touch.

Finally, I'd like to see more LIS professors have some of their office hours in an open setting—commenting, sharing, and moving the conversation forward. I love what I see from Scott Nicholson's (professor of game design and development, Wilfrid Laurier University, Brantford, Ontario) YouTube videos and online classes on gaming.[1] The late Laurel Ann Clyde (former LIS professor, University of Iceland, Reykjavik) wrote about the use of blogs in libraries and admonished librarians to take advantage of the medium.[2] To paraphrase her, "By not taking advantage of the opportunities for discussion, exchange, and learning among students, professors, and the greater global LIS community, libraries will surely suffer."

NOTES

1. Scott Nicholson, http://scottnicholson.com/.
2. Laurel Ann Clyde, *Weblogs and Libraries* (Oxford: Chandos, 2004).

STUCK IN THE PAST

"I LIKE BOOKS." This is one answer to the introductory question I ask when meeting a class for the first time: "What brings you to librarianship?" The answers vary just as LIS students do, whether they're recent college graduates or those returning to school for a second career in libraries. The "books" answer begs the question, "Do you mean the content or the container?" Students starting graduate school who want to work in libraries with stacks filled with books may be aiming for the wrong profession.

Archives and rare books collections will always need librarians to curate and preserve, but the shift within public and academic libraries of late may mean a very different set of duties not revolving entirely around the containers so many of us love. Case in point: at a recent dinner with three academic library directors, all detailed plans to move more and more of their book and print journal collections to storage facilities to make additional space for students to study and collaborate.

The book–library connection isn't limited to wannabe librarians; it's the public's view, as well. OCLC's study, "Perceptions of Libraries, 2010," reports that the number of people who associate the word *library* with books has risen to 75 percent—up from 69 percent in 2005.[1] As Borders stores have closed around the country and e-reader popularity soars, we need to focus on what comes next in the evolution of our services.

FINDING THINGS

Another answer I get to my question is, "I like to find things," implying this future librarian sees herself at a reference desk pointing people toward the very best information for their needs. While some of us focus on authority or the "best information," OCLC has reported that people turn to search engines first, not to the anxious reference librarian standing by in the library. The most recent report states that 1 percent of people surveyed began their information search at a library website.[2] Yet, in many libraries, those web redesign committee meetings just keep chugging along, producing the same types of websites operating from the same false assumptions. (For more on this, read Aaron Schmidt's "Resist That Redesign.")[3]

The researchers also found that "ask an expert" sites have grown substantially. In 2005, only 15 percent of respondents said they used such sites; in 2010, 43 percent.[4] Meanwhile, "ask a librarian" services have remained flat.[5] This is another one of those difficult truths: people do not think of the library first when they need information no matter how much we may enjoy the thrill of the hunt for the best, most complete answer. However, the new report notes that 83 percent of people who have used a librarian for search assistance perceived added value. The number jumps to 88 percent among those identifying themselves as economically impacted.[6]

DOING THINGS

Instead of finding things, how about doing things? How about creating localized collections of our most unique stuff and, more importantly, helping our library users to do the same? Watching the HarperCollins/Overdrive e-book license limitation kerfuffle leads me to imagine a future where libraries gather, produce, and curate content in ways only beginning to be explored that bypass the traditional author-to-publisher-to-library-to-reader model we've worked with for decades.[7]

Reflecting on OCLC's numbers for people who turn to library websites first when seeking information means we need to get reference librarians out of libraries and into the places where they might best help people—both in physical space and virtually. Who's to say we can't embed ourselves in the expert sites too? Check out the "Slam the Boards" initiatives by Arlington Heights Memorial Library's Bill Pardue (a 2011 *LJ* Mover & Shaker) and other librarians to see this in play at answer sites.[8]

It's not out of the question to imagine these service models based on community enrichment and building connections. We need a course in library school devoted to teaching people to build spaces both physical and virtual for constituents to come together. We need to prioritize marketing and branding these spaces and services consistently. Doing so will help us in creating, maintaining, and evaluating the information commons. The commons, a vital part of what our spaces can be, is strengthened by each person who makes use of it. The Digital Media Lab at Skokie Public Library, Illinois, is a perfect example of space devoted to content creation for users.[9]

There's a cadre of LIS students coming up who would jump at the chance for jobs in digital media labs or the information commons. Before that can happen, however, library leadership must move beyond the lending/reference model to a broader view of what's possible in a community-based space focused on helping people.

What's one of the best answers I've ever gotten to my question? "I want to change people's lives."

NOTES

1. Brad Gauder, "Perceptions of Libraries, 2010: Context and Community," *OCLC*, 2011, 38, www.oclc.org/content/dam/oclc/reports/2010perceptions/2010perceptions_all.pdf.
2. Ibid., 32.
3. Aaron Schmidt, "Resist That Redesign," *Library Journal: The User Experience*, March 1, 2010, http://lj.libraryjournal.com/2010/03/opinion/aaron-schmidt/resist-that-redesign-the-user-experience/#_.
4. Gauder, "Perceptions of Libraries, 2010: Context and Community," 33, www.oclc.org/content/dam/oclc/reports/2010perceptions/2010perceptions_all.pdf.
5. Ibid., 95.
6. Ibid., 42.
7. Digital Shift, www.thedigitalshift.com/2012/02/ebooks/one-year-later-harpercollins-sticking-to-26-loan-cap-and-some-librarians-rethink-opposition/.
8. Bill Pardue, "Movers & Shakers 2011," *Library Journal*, http://lj.libraryjournal.com/2011/03/people/movers-shakers-2011/bill-pardue-movers-shakers-2011-change-agents/; Facebook, https://www.facebook.com/groups/9325045378/?notif_t=group_r2j.
9. Skokie Public Library, https://skokielibrary.info/services/computers-technology/digital-media-labs/.

ONLINE LIS EDUCATION—OR NOT

AFTER JOINING SAN José State University's (SJSU) all-online LIS program, I read with great interest the report from Pew Internet & American Life, "The Digital Revolution and Higher Education."[1] Pew interviewed over 1,000 college presidents and more than 2,100 members of the general public. One of the key findings: only 29 percent of the public says online courses offer an equal value compared with courses taken in a classroom. Half (51 percent) of the college presidents surveyed say online courses provide the same value.[2] I'd like to see a similar survey focused specifically on LIS education. Would students—such as at SJSU, Drexel, or other completely online LIS programs—rate their online experience as equal in value to face-to-face instruction?

That depends on the caliber of the online experience. Are the classes just ported over from face-to-face syllabi and entirely text-based? Read, respond, repeat. Many students frown upon this style of online course. I wonder how many of the general public respondents had the mostly text-based correspondence-style classes, or if emerging technologies and the social web were used to enhance their coursework.

Also, 50 percent of college presidents "predict that ten years from now most of their students will take classes online."[3] In our field, more programs will put at least part of their courses online if they haven't already done so.

ONLINE OR NOT

The decision to pursue a graduate library degree involves multiple considerations: time, money, and location are but a few. Despite the views and predictions of college presidents and the lower ratings for online education from the general public, many library school candidates will still choose online over on campus. After all, online offerings mean that students are not tied geographically to just the school in their own state. Before applying to an online program, however, prospective grad students need to do some comparative shopping and soul-searching.

First, evaluate a program's curriculum. Does it reflect current issues and trends in the profession? Does it include a focus on core values and emerging technologies? Can you examine a course catalog and a schedule of current offerings? What's the process for the ongoing evolution of the curriculum itself? These things should be transparent and easy to find on the school's website. The website is also indicative of the school's attitudes and perceptions as to how the Web can be used to share information.

Second, reflect on your learning style and comfort level with technology before making a decision. Is course delivery via face-to-face in the physical classroom, a hybrid model of boot camp-style days followed by online exercises for the rest of the semester, or entirely online? Whatever your learning style, tech skills and comfort are paramount for success in today's libraries and information environments.

Third, do your research! Search for posts about the school on the Web. Blogs including Hack Library School and student blogs may offer insights beyond the marketing efforts of the schools being considered.[4] Search the archives of *Library Journal* and look for mention of the program in the ALA's directory for accredited programs.[5] The degree is a high price tag decision—make it carefully.

ONLINE ASSETS

I may have a bit of a bias, but I would much rather my students make the short trip to their desks and computers instead of commuting across town or farther. Time saved on travel could roll over into time spent on coursework or finding a balance between school, work, and life. Money saved on gas and travel could transform into paying for classes or student loans.

Other students may be drawn to the classroom, to in-person interaction with a professor and other classmates. I would argue, however, that the technologies available at San José State that allow me to lecture, interact with, and guide my students rival those classrooms. My weekly drop-in office hours via web conferencing software give students a chance to ask a question or just say hi. An integrated instant messaging program automatically populates class tabs with my student rosters, so faculty and students can exchange quick messages.

Reflecting on Pew's data, there is no excuse for online education to be rated below face-to-face if students and faculty have access to technologies that not only replicate but enhance the learning experience. In reality, however, there are certain appurtenances and hurdles to consider in e-learning environments. Can we truly re-create all that is well and good in face-to-face classrooms? Are there some things that technology simply can't overcome? For potential LIS students pondering online, research and reflection should influence the decision, no matter what the Pew data says.

NOTES

1. Kim Parker, Amanda Lenhart, and Kathleen Moore, "The Digital Revolution and Higher Education: College Presidents, Public Differ on Value of Online Learning," Pew Research Center's Internet & American Life Project, August 28, 2011, www.pewinternet.org/files/old-media//Files/Reports/2011/PIP-Online-Learning.pdf.
2. Ibid., 1.
3. Ibid.
4. *Hack Library School*, http://hacklibraryschool.com.
5. *Library Journal*, http://lj.libraryjournal.com; www.ala.org/accreditedprograms/directory.

BEST OF BOTH WORLDS

AN LIS STUDENT'S letter to the editor of *Library Journal* gave me pause. Krystal Taylor, studying at Indiana University–Purdue University Indianapolis, detailed the move her program was making from classroom-based instruction to almost 100 percent online delivery.[1] A big picture concern is evident: "What cost will this be to the library and information science field?" Her word for those completing an online master's of library science: *lackluster*.

I have more than a passing interest in this change. Yes, it's indicative of a major shift in LIS education, but my interest is also a personal one. I teach via the San José State University online program, and I graduated from Indiana University's (IU's) LIS program in 1995. Back then I took classes on the IU South Bend campus one or two nights a week with adjuncts or via closed-circuit TV and a phone system that linked my fellow students and me to the classroom. One summer, I drove 200-plus miles each way for three weekends to take "Fiscal Responsibility in Libraries" at the Bloomington campus. Many, I'm sure, had a similar experience.

TURNING THE TIDE

Taylor writes, "Having taken both types of courses, I am convinced that face-to-face [F2F] courses are the better option."[2] I might argue the tide is turning on that sentiment. Other programs have announced online library degrees (e.g., University of Southern California). Frankly, a brick-and-mortar LIS school without a fully online option may become a quaint reminder of days gone by in the next decade. With this shift comes a few important considerations for the various stakeholders: students, faculty, hiring librarians, and accrediting bodies.

Students will have more choices of schools, but those will most probably be online. I appreciate Taylor's candor in her letter as she worries about the loss of passion in the field.[3] F2F discussions and debates in the classroom can be truly exhilarating. Those with a similar concern might explore some of the newer methods of online learning to see what's possible with emerging technologies. Attend a free webinar, try out a MOOC, or explore the bleeding edge of library communities by participating on Twitter #libchats or the thriving "Library Related People" group on Facebook, 3,000-plus global library folk strong.[4] I promise: passion is present there.

Faculty moving from F2F to online should seek out best practices in online learning. Remember: text-based lectures and text-based discussion forums are not a twenty-first-century model. I've learned that my students respond positively when they see and hear me via short presentations recorded with Panopto. That they can respond via their blogs, video, audio, or in our weekly chats as part of class discussion adds to the interaction.

LIS educators will need to revamp assignments and rubrics. I would suggest assignments that allow for a broad range of creativity and exploration. What might have been, "Write an eight-page paper on new types of literacies for young people" might become, "Create a synthesis of recent research and thinking about new literacies for young people via the delivery channel of your choice: video, audio, etc." Assessment would include a statute that addresses the mode of presentation *and* synthesis of the topic.

Hiring librarians may find with more LIS programs online that they have choices of candidates from all sorts of programs across the United States and beyond. A new hire in youth service may come from a highly regarded children's program far away, while a user experience job may go to someone from a thriving technology-focused program nearby. The negative view of staffing a local library from the local library school fades when local hires are more globally educated.

KEEPING PACE WITH CHANGE

Our accrediting bodies must consider these changes as well. Paul LeBlanc's piece at *EDUCAUSE Review,* "Thinking about Accreditation in a Rapidly Changing World," includes this response to the question of classroom learning versus online: "the question of fifteen years ago—'How can we make online learning the equal of traditionally delivered learning?'—has been reversed. We now ask, 'How can we make traditionally delivered learning the equal of the best-designed online learning?' This is because disruptive innovations always start as inferior to incumbent models."[5] LeBlanc explores some important ideas about accreditation in a time of great change within higher education. Can we evaluate online programs the same way we've evaluated traditional F2F delivery? He urges, "Accreditors need to think about their relationship to innovation. If the standards are built largely to assess incumbent models and are enforced by incumbents, they must be—by their very nature—conservative and in service to the status quo."[6]

As more LIS schools move online, the opportunities for library education to emerge as dynamic, thought-provoking, and innovative multiply with every new option. Even so, the modality isn't as important as the students and professors giving it their all.

NOTES

1. Krystal Taylor, "Lackluster LIS Program," *Library Journal: Letters to LJ,* March 22, 2013, http://lj.libraryjournal.com/2013/03/opinion/feedback-letters-to-lj-march-15–2013-issue/.
2. Ibid.
3. Ibid.
4. "Library Related People," Facebook, https://www.facebook.com/groups/libraryrelatedpeeps/.

5. Paul J. LeBlanc, "Thinking about Accreditation in a Rapidly Changing World," *EDUCAUSE Review,* April 1, 2013, http://er.educause.edu/articles/2013/4/thinking-about-accreditation-in-a-rapidly-changing-world.
6. Ibid.

PROFESSIONALISM MATTERS

AS AN LIS educator, I get to grade electronic portfolios for a cadre of students. The portfolio is part of their culminating experience at San José State University and serves as a lexicon of learning, detailing experiences and evidence of their mastery of our competencies. It promotes a high degree of self-evaluation by articulating a statement of professional philosophy. Truth be told, both students and practitioners can benefit from careful consideration of what it means to be a professional in libraries.

A CROWDED FIELD

In a market where one library job may have 200 applicants, how do you set yourself apart? Demonstrating skills is one way. A well-crafted cover letter outlining pertinent experience and pointers to an e-portfolio or online vita with links to a social networking presence and other evidence is a good start. For sample cover letters that work, see "Open Cover Letters," the brainchild of *Library Journal* Mover & Shaker Stephen X. Flynn.[1] Focusing on professionalism, foundational values, and service throughout all of these resources can set you apart. No library experience? Seek out an internship or volunteer opportunity to establish some evidence of your own contributions to the field.

MODEL ONLINE BEHAVIOR

Professionalism matters online just as much as it matters in the physical library or information workplace. As a professor, I can model the characteristics of a professional to my students online via our interactions in class chat, my lectures, blogging, and Twitter.[2] But my students are also learning from those they meet virtually. If you are a professional participating in online conversations, be aware that you are influencing the next wave of librarians even before they graduate.

QUALITY OVER QUANTITY

A student recently asked if she should include the number of Twitter followers she has on her résumé as she applied for a technology position. I advised that a carefully worded statement about her experience participating, teaching, and sharing online might make for a better selling point than citing those figures. I reminded her of a blog post from Seth Godin that included this advice for up-and-comers: "There's no limit now. No limit to how many clicks, readers, followers, and friends you can acquire. . . . Instead of getting better, you focus obsessively on getting bigger . . . Compared to what? You're never going to be the biggest, so it seems like being better is a reasonable alternative."[3] I urged her to provide substantive details of what she could bring to the job instead of an indication of her reach.

The online world so easily becomes a popularity contest. Folks fall over themselves to get retweeted, liked, linked, and noticed. Sometimes it feels like a weird, online version of high school. I'm more interested in those folks who are working hard, with little notice, day in and day out, to enact change within their communities. Teen librarian Justin Hoenke, a contributor to my blog Tame the Web, shared a success story with me: one of his teens recently gained U.S. citizenship.

CONTRIBUTIONS MATTER

Lasting contributions can be made online. It does not matter where you write, but you must write professionally and with an eye toward the future. I still return to seminal blog posts such as Karen Schneider's, "The User Is Not Broken," as well as other blog posts, *LJ* articles, and studies that have inspired me.[4] Professional writing, no matter whether it's on a blog, in a professional journal, or an academic paper, should always be of the highest caliber.

The nature of professional contributions, however, is broader than just mass appeal on blogs or Twitter.

FRAMING THE FUTURE

Defining one's approach to professional contributions should begin in library school. One section of our e-portfolio asks students to summarize how they will contribute to the cultural, economic, educational, and social well-being of their communities. The act of writing this frames students' future work around the people they will serve.

I recall a writing exercise as part of a staff development day right after I finished my master's of library science degree. Looking back, I realize now I was being asked to craft my own professional philosophy. Later, when I moved to LIS education, I was asked to articulate my philosophy of teaching. If you haven't done an exercise like this, give it a try and ask yourself: what is your current professional philosophy? Include a focus on who you serve (the public or internal staff), how you will contribute to the purpose of your specific workplace or environment, and how you will continue to learn. Find your professional focus and stick to it, developing it as you go.

Let your actions speak louder than your words, however: professionalism matters, while popularity is illusory, fleeting, and short-lived. Your contributions to the field, by enhancing service, creating new models to replace outdated practice, and quietly working to improve communities, matter most.

NOTES

1. "Open Cover Letters," *Library Journal*, http://opencoverletters.com; http://lj.libraryjournal.com/2012/03/people/movers-shakers-2012/stephen-x-flynn-movers-shakers-2012-tech-leaders/.
2. Michael Stephens, Twitter, https://twitter.com/mstephens7.
3. Seth Godin, "Infinity—They Keep Making More of It," April 29, 2009, *SethGodin.Typepad.com*, http://sethgodin.typepad.com/seths_blog/2009/04/infinitythey-keep-making-more-of-it.html.
4. Karen G. Schneider, "The User Is Not Broken: A Meme Masquerading as a Manifesto," *Free Range Librarian*, June 3, 2006, http://freerangelibrarian.com/2006/06/03/the-user-is-not-broken-a-meme-masquerading-as-a-manifesto/.

SEEK A CHALLENGE

DANIEL CHUDNOV, CURRENTLY the director of scholarly technology at George Washington University, once wrote a blog post, "Advice to a Library School Student," for *One Big Library*. He wrote:

> The best advice anybody ever gave me when I was finishing library school and looking for a job was "look at all your options and choose the most challenging one. If it scares you, like you think maybe you won't be up to the challenge, you're on the right track and should go for it." If you don't feel challenged now, you're right to be looking elsewhere (especially if you're young or don't otherwise have lots of obligations to other people and can freely look around).[1]

The current economic climate may impact "looking elsewhere" for many librarians already employed, but for recent graduates who can move anywhere, this is sound advice. You'll immediately better your chances to land a job. More important, however, is the idea of seeking a challenge.

SLACKERS NOT WANTED

At a recent focus group for a research project for the EDUCAUSE Learning Initiatives conference, a small group of librarians and library information technology support staff shared their insights about the changing educational landscape. They all agreed that the requirements for supporting a university's mission are changing, just as our students are changing. One librarian noted a particular challenge: "Some librarians are coasting to retirement—they've checked out."

Coasting, in library school and in our jobs, is not an option. Sending students who have coasted through their LIS program to your library to coast perpetuates this problem. I can tell which students are merely sailing through their program, just as I can tell when a professor has "checked out" of his or her own job.

Students: are you doing the bare minimum in your LIS program? Are you turning in "good enough" papers that show no excitement, curiosity, or passion for librarianship? Or are you going above and beyond the expectations of your teachers? You get what you bring to your program.

We can't force you to learn or open your mind to the future possibilities of libraries. And yes, you may get an okay or better grade for just coasting, depending on your teacher; grade inflation is alive and well in many LIS programs. A friend and colleague said of such slackers, "The field can't afford them; I don't want to teach them." Amen.

THIS MEANS PROFESSORS, TOO

Professors, have you updated your syllabi lately? Are you still using readings and views of LIS from 1985? Have you changed your assignments to reflect current practice and emerging research about information behavior that excite and engage your charges? Some of the tried and true will always be valuable, but some of it may no longer work in today's (and tomorrow's) libraries, where the focus is on new trends, new tech, and new ideas.

The onus for change lies with both students and LIS faculty. Students should provide constructive evaluations of their learning experience. Faculty should respond with curricular changes and updated course offerings as quickly as possible. Library school administration should enable these conversations about change in an open, transparent process. LIS programs must be nimble and quick if they are to survive in the current economy.

STILL LEARNING

I have a little plaque in my office I purchased in England, quoting Michelangelo: "I am still learning." I tell my students that the minute I stop learning, I need to pack up my office and go sell tomatoes on the highway somewhere.

Roy Tennant (*Library Journal* blogger and Web4Lib moderator) has some wonderful insights on this, including, "Learn as you breathe. You breathe all the time without even thinking about it. That is how you must learn."[2]

For those who have "checked out" of their library jobs, what would bring you back? Have you lost sight of why you got into librarianship in the first place? Have you stopped bringing your heart with you to work?

You owe it to your users to be competent, engaged, and always learning professionals. Imagine a challenge that would excite you, and go talk to your manager about it. Challenge yourself as well: explore that new web technology on your own, long before official training is offered.

I applaud the student who e-mails me before classes start to say she's taking my web design class because it's new and scary but necessary for her education. I applaud the librarian who takes on a difficult new project as a way to keep his professional fires burning. What challenge will you seek out today? How will you continue to learn? Maybe next to my "still learning" plaque, I'll place a Post-it as another reminder: "Find your next challenge."

NOTES

1. Daniel Chudnov, "Advice to a Library School Student," *One Big Library,* October 21, 2010.
2. Web4Lib, http://web4lib.org; Roy Tennant, "Managing Personal Change," *Library Journal: The Digital Shift,* September 29, 2010, www.thedigitalshift. com/2010/09/roy-tennant-digital-libraries/managing-personal-change/.

THE POWER OF QUIET

HAVE YOU EVER sat in a meeting and wished silently that the person holding the floor would *shut up?* Would you prefer quiet time to get work done to a talky decision-making session? If so, you may be an introvert.

AN INNER WORLD

Author Susan Cain explores this topic in *Quiet: The Power of Introverts in a World That Can't Stop Talking,* a title that resonated deeply with me.[1] Cain notes that there is no modern-day definition for what it means to be introverted; Carl Jung's 1921 definition—drawn to the inner world of thought and feeling—seems limited.[2] Cain argues that society honors the extroverted more. Synthesizing recent research, Cain offers this: "introverts and extroverts differ in the level of outside stimulation they need to function well. Introverts feel 'just right' with less stimulation, as when they sip wine with a close friend, solve a crossword puzzle, or read a book."[3]

Sound familiar? Yes, but it must be said that we can turn it on when needed. According to Cain, it's possible for introverts to act like extroverts for work, people they love, or anything they value. She urges those on the introverted side not only to embrace their introversion but to seek ways to enhance our brief forays into extroversion. Those "extro-adventures" should prove rewarding, the fruits of what Cain calls "deliberate practice."[4]

RECHARGING AND REACHING OUT

I'll own it: I was painfully shy all through school and into my library career; I'm much more at home with smaller groups and quiet discussion. I prefer chunks of alone time to reflect and prepare. When I tell people I identify as an introvert, they say, "How are you able to give speeches in front of six hundred people and still consider yourself an introvert?" Introverts, I say, know how to "bring it," or at least can learn when we have to. Learning how to embrace your "inner extrovert" when you need to is necessary. But it has a cost.

I confessed this during a recent talk, telling the folks in the ballroom that soon after my presentation, I'd be curled in a ball on the floor of my hotel room, recharging for the next event. An only child, I've also shared many an "a-ha" moment with other "onlies" in our field.

Someone adept at deliberate practice or mindfulness might learn that the superpowers of the introvert can prove most beneficial when the time comes to play "pretend extrovert," such as by speaking up once in every meeting, giving a lightning talk at a local conference, or going out of the way to talk to library patrons once per day. Have you done it?

Take a look at Oregon's Multnomah County Public Library's "My Librarian" page for inspiration.[5] This glimpse of the staff is not steeped in "Oh, look, we're not shushing" or attempts to be overly cool that reek of desperation. It's real folks from all walks of life sharing themselves. I can't tell if Edna K. or Eric G. are introverts or extroverts, but does it matter? They are putting themselves front and center for library users, making themselves available for personalized recommendations of books, media, and more. Edna K. says it best: "I got mad respect for anybody trying to make a difference in this world. Reach out and touch, your Librarian is ready to share."[6] Take a look at the Johnson County Library, Overland Park, Kansas, staff page to see another photographic example.[7]

STRIKE A BALANCE

Cain's book illuminates another important issue: how introverts and extroverts learn and interact. For those managing a varied staff, it's good to recognize that some will require individual time to process new ideas, while others thrive in the chaos of a busy institution.

Two people can have the same plan, but their style differences make other staff think they have opposing viewpoints and end points. Their personality types create assorted paths to the same goal. They communicate diversely. We need to build into our processes, our tools, ways to manage that divergence. In projects, we need open communication, question-and-answer sessions, and statements of purpose that allow for those very different styles of planning and leadership.

Turn the concept outward, and it's time to consider how to balance the needs of patrons seeking quiet and those seeking a socially charged collaborative experience. When working on a new building or renovation, examine the spaces you are creating. Is there room for both quiet reflection and audible activity? Is there a place where the two can meet?

It's been too easy to argue for more extroverts in our field, more individuals who can staff a reference point, teach classes, and advocate loudly for the community. Honoring our innate traits—introvert or extrovert—and learning from one another seems like a more balanced goal. Understand and appreciate the differences in how each of us interacts and what we can bring to the table.

NOTES

1. Susan Cain, *Quiet: The Power of Introverts in a World That Can't Stop Talking* (New York: Crown Publishing, 2012).
2. Ibid., 10.
3. Ibid., 11.
4. Ibid.
5. "My Librarian," Multnomah County Public Library, https://multcolib.org/my-librarian.
6. Multnomah County Public Library, https://multcolib.org/users/edna-k.
7. Johnson County Public Library, http://jocolibrary.org/about/staff.

COMMUNITIES OF PRACTICE

A S A PROFESSION, we need to believe in ourselves and use that feeling of worth to build close-knit communities within LIS and outside it. Forging strong relationships with other professionals at events and online can provide learning opportunities as well as changes in mind-set. As with most of the topics I explore in my writing and teaching, conversation is king. Conferences can be a great way to enliven our library communities, especially conferences that go beyond sit-and-listen models to interactive, team-building, innovation-inspiring models that prompt in-depth discussion.

I was struck by the tight-knit community of information professionals during a trip to New Zealand to keynote their annual meeting. Conversations about service, our users, and more flowed freely with librarians, vendors, and others playing key roles. This felt different and invigorating.

Within these communities, we also need to build better mentoring relationships. The mentee and the mentor could gain so much, as the former brings a fresh perspective to the profession, and the latter brings know-how and wisdom from years of experience. LIS students would benefit from multiple types of mentors: LIS professors, front-line librarians, and administrators.

One way we build community is through scholarly conversation, but too often this conversation gets stymied behind a pay wall. We need to be more proactive at sharing research through new channels such as blogs, podcasts, and tweets.

Communities form when we open our doors and ask people to participate in our work. Communities form when we extend not only our reach, but our hearts. It is possible to build communities that bridge cultures and geographical space.

NOTES FROM SOME SMALL ISLANDS

I WAS HONORED to give one of the keynote addresses at the 2013 Library and Information Association of New Zealand Aotearoa (LIANZA) conference. There, I met many New Zealand (NZ) LIS professionals and got a glimpse of how they work. I also became intimately acquainted with the integration of Maori culture into New Zealander LIS professionals' lives. The Maori are the original citizens of the two islands.

The conference began with a *powhiri* at Turangawaewae Marae, a sacred place near Hamilton that is the traditional home of the Maori king. The *powhiri* ceremony involves welcoming newcomers to the Marae, a dialogue between Maori hosts and the visitors, a donation (*koha*) to the group, shared singing, and the opportunity to touch noses with the elders, known as a *hongi*, which signifies the joining of the two groups.

I was a bit hesitant about touching noses with the line of elders, but when a lovely lady grabbed my hands and pulled me in, I was sold. It felt special and right to be welcomed in this manner. The nose-touching gave way to afternoon tea, chat, and a keynote address in the auditorium. This was the most unique, culturally significant, and inclusive welcome to a conference I'd ever attended.

SOCIAL NETWORKING

I was reminded of Tom Standage's new book, *Writing on the Wall: Social Media—The First 2,000 Years,* in which he argues that social media is nothing new, with papyrus scrolls and Twitter both examples of instant mass communication tools.[1] The *hongi* tradition, how two groups come together pulling everyone in to the same community, made me think this is also evidence of pre-Internet social networking.

I found LIANZA 2013 to be a positive and encouraging experience. Keynote addresses, mine included, ended with a traditional Maori song (*waiata*). Teatime offered a chance for folks to network and browse exhibits. At what was billed on the LIANZA site as "the legendary conference dinner," delegates were on their feet cutting a rug before dessert was even served. Delegates and vendors appeared in costume to match the "Take Me to the River" theme.

A CLOSE COMMUNITY

Something struck me about this conference, in addition to my interactions with the library folk I met as we traveled down the North Island, stopping in Wellington for a talk I gave at Victoria University and on to the South Island. At a combination #hyperlibMOOC and library folk tweetup held at Pomeroy's Pub in Christchurch, I finally asked the assembled group, "Why does the LIS community here feel so cohesive and tight-knit? Is it the isolation?" Between the pub chat and the question I threw out to Kiwis in my Twitter network, the ideas flowed:

"Tight-knit for sure, but many local authorities in NZ are becoming smaller, and there are fewer employing authorities, so librarians are working in larger organizations and tend to meet one another more often," said Brendon Moir, system analyst for digital library services at Christchurch City Libraries. "The local and national partnerships between libraries have become really important, and this will only increase."

Cath Sheard, assistant manager for cultural services at the South Taranaki District Council, thought it's a "relatively small pool of people to get collegial support from, so people tend to form strong bonds." She also cautioned, though, that "small country, people in a smallish profession need to be 'nice'—speak badly of someone, it gets round. Think two degrees of sep[aration], not six." Sally

Pewhairangi, who at the time worked at the Waimakariri Libraries, echoed this thought: It is "difficult to speak out against policy, actions, etc., because it will be remembered."

I felt the closeness when I spoke with vendors on the LIANZA exhibit floor. NZ Micrographic Services strives for "a close and intimate relationship with the GLAM [galleries, libraries, archives, and museums] sector," Andy Fenton, managing director, told me. "We have always chosen to treat customers as friends and colleagues— you'd do your best never to let them down, right?" Fenton told me that his core values include "give a lot to gain a little" and "treat everyone like a good friend or neighbor." Transparency from vendors and commiseration evident on the conference floor were heartening.

SELF-RELIANCE

There is a desire to participate in the greater LIS community, but the reality of their geographic location has forced our colleagues in NZ to be more self-reliant. Here, the power of large-scale online learning such as the Australian and NZ (ANZ) 23 Mobile Things and the Hyperlinked Library MOOC have given places like NZ a pipeline to the community that it never had before.[2] However, doing some things on our own can be rewarding.

Take a lesson from this small island nation. Perhaps the global library community itself needs to stop questioning our worth and holding up "saints and sages" to profess it and, instead, have professional self-esteem that is based upon our intrinsic value and not on an external power.

NOTES

1. Tom Standage, *Writing on the Wall: Social Media—The First 2,000 Years* (New York: Bloomsbury Publishing, 2013).
2. 23 Mobile Things, https://anz23mobilethings.wordpress.com.

THE ROLE OF MENTORING

HAVING A STRONG mentor during your first few years as a librarian can provide a safety net of advice, encouragement, and caution for a newly minted professional. Such a relationship would be even better if it began during LIS education. This would also serve to diminish the perceived divide between practice and library schools. In fact, mentoring up-and-coming professionals, those who will inherit the changed, and changing, landscape of libraries, should be one of the values of librarianship.

Is it worthwhile to formalize this process on both sides of practice and LIS? Could students be aligned with practicing librarians within their area of interest early on and continue to rely on them throughout the coursework, job search, and first hire? Such initiatives could be local, within a school, or could even stretch worldwide, enhanced by technologies such as Skype. Let's look at some of the benefits of mentoring.

THE VALUE OF MENTORING

Mentors can advise new librarians on all aspects of the profession, including tips for getting along with coworkers, the ins and outs of dealing with library administrators, and the like. The online world offers a new twist. While much is gained by participating in the ubiquitous social networks, there are pitfalls as well. A professional's expressions are now open for the world to read, hear, or view. Because anyone tweeting, blogging, or Facebooking can share their thoughts so easily and post sometimes without thought, a strong mentor who guides students or new grads in the ways of online life could help make or break a career.

I was lucky in my years at the public library to have had several mentors who pushed, prodded, and helped prioritize things for me as I discovered technology, blogging, and the social web. As I moved into teaching, I became a de facto mentor for many of our new hires or for those interested in going to library school. I found playing both roles, mentee and mentor, to be rewarding. They contrasted with my own master's program in the 1990s, which afforded little opportunity for finding a mentor. Nor do I recall much mention of the process or the role a mentor could play in one's professional life.

Mentoring is different from the type of advising many LIS students receive, which is usually of the "Which classes should I take next?" variety. Yes, it is possible to slide through a library program without speaking more than a few words to an advisor, but quality advising can become a form of mentoring and improve the educational experience.

BENEFITS FOR PROFS

It is easy to pay lip service to "networking opportunities" such as receptions, open houses, and other social events during library school, but how many true mentor relationships are established there? It takes a certain type of student—extroverted for sure—and a certain type of mentor—one who has the time, patience, and motivation to serve. In a profession that has historically attracted introverts, this relationship is indeed hard to form. In addition, many librarians are doing more work than ever before bowing to economic pressures, and it becomes a perfect storm of "no time, too shy."

What of library school professors? Joe Hardenbrook offered some advice about library school at his Mr. Library Dude blog: "Get a mentor! Someone who is a working librarian. Not a library school professor who hasn't worked in libraries for 20 years."[1] It's a criticism I've heard before—LIS professors are out of touch with true practice. Maybe the mentoring should go both ways. Profs should get on the front lines every so often with the person they're mentoring—that way, both learn. The same could be said for participation online. Those not familiar with social sites might learn from their students. In turn, a discussion about ethics and values in one's online life might prevent embarrassment or worse.

Administrators could play a role as well. As such, students and new grads learn not only on the front line but from behind the scenes, too. That's where funding issues come into play, where you learn how the tough decisions are made, and where you see the mandate administrators always have to balance cost with customer service and politics. It's easy for front-line staff to criticize, but it's a different thing altogether when they learn what goes on in administration. The shape of this process is circular: students learning the front lines and the administration's side, administration renewing themselves on the front line, and LIS professors also relearning (or learning) front-line skills and perhaps refreshing on the administration side.

Most of the time when we hear about mentoring in librarianship, the word *informal* is attached. Could a formalized process work, or is mentoring a more organic thing that grows from like-mindedness and a comfort built over time? Let's start creating these connections for students (and for profs and administrators) and move to formalize the process.

NOTE

1. Joe Hardenbrook, "'I Graduated from a Top Library School.' Yeah, So What?" *Mr. Library Dude,* July 21, 2011, https://mrlibrarydude.wordpress.com/2011/07/21/i-graduated-from-a-top-library-school-yeah-so-what/.

AGE OF PARTICIPATION

IT'S THE MUSEUM director's conundrum. She has six brief seconds to grab the visitor's attention as they walk past each exhibit. Once they pass the exhibit, they're gone for good. That thought went through my mind as I stood talking with a museum administrator at a *Stammtisch* in Berlin in March 2010. Could adding a social, participatory component to museum exhibitions maximize this brief window of opportunity?

I couldn't help but think that libraries face this same problem. How can we grab the public's interest despite the one-click availability of information? How can we compete with the seductive voice of Siri?

I revisited these questions and more at the Salzburg Global Seminar program, "Libraries and Museums in an Era of Participatory

Culture," held October 19–23, 2011, and cosponsored by the Institute of Museum and Library Services.[1] Representatives from over twenty countries gathered for five intensive days of discussion and deliberations about the future of cultural institutions in a time of hyperconnected social participation.

Building collections and seeking ways to engage the public and promote curiosity challenge us all. The seminar gave me a new-found appreciation for the work of museum professionals and cultural institutions. The era of participatory culture demands that cultural and information professionals play an active, visible role in our communities. My takeaways were many.

MORE ACCESS

Breaking down barriers remains a goal for all. Transparency and access can lead to demonstrating the value of our institutions to the public. Gary Vikan, who recently retired as director of the Walters Art Museum in Baltimore, described dropping admission fees to encourage visits, resulting in an increase.[2] Walls between visitors and museum staff became windows that curators could open to talk directly with the public. "Everything we do should be measured by the benefit [to] the public," he said. What fees might libraries drop? What walls could become windows into the operation of the library?

Preserving a community's digital heritage is the work of both libraries and museums, but involving the community in these efforts is imperative as we move forward. Gathering histories via various media, scanning documents and objects for sharing online, and other activities are an important consideration for future services. A library in Colombia made it a service priority to invite people to bring in their documents and photos for digitization, adding Creative Commons licenses to the materials. A museum in India gave people an opportunity to display their personal collections in museum space. Folks could even co-curate their objects with museum staff.

WHERE LEARNING OCCURS

These participatory spaces are where learning will occur. Pablo Andrade, directorate of libraries, archives, and museums in Santiago, Chile, described the thriving virtual community created for residents of Chile. A key phrase impressed me in a video about the project: "all of them communicating every day in the community of local content."[3] Not only are participants creating, curating, and sharing, they are exchanging knowledge without curriculum and administrators.

Truly, the world has become flatter. Understanding and empathy among cross-cultural partners in a technological environment is the key to success. Technology doesn't solve our problems, but it can be a conduit to making change and promoting progress. Noha Adly, deputy head of the information and technology sector at Bibliotheca Alexandria in Egypt, illustrated this concept when she described the fast-growing digital collection her library was amassing around the Egyptian revolution: 2.8 million tweets, 90,000 videos, 230,000 images, 18,000 Facebook pages.

WHEN A GUEST BECOMES A HOST

Finally, I also took away the knowledge that my own emphasis on humanism and the heart in my teaching is an important part of what comes next. All of the talks and group reports at the seminar shared that common thread. Words such as *civility, sharing,* and *caring* were used throughout the program. Across our communities and across cultures, understanding, empathy, and kindness matter in everything we do. Technology extends human reach but participation requires engaged participants who feel welcome, comfortable, and valued. Serhan Ada, head of the cultural management program of Istanbul Bilgi University, summed it up well in a final comment: "Participation occurs when someone welcomed as a guest feels as though they have become a host."

That's an important consideration in our evolution as cultural institutions: how will we open the door and invite everyone inside to participate?

NOTES

1. "Libraries and Museums in an Era of Participatory Culture," www.spnhc.org/media/assets/SGS_Report_2012.pdf.
2. Walters Art Museum, http://thewalters.org/news/releases/article.aspx?e_id=362.
3. YouTube, https://www.youtube.com/watch?feature=player_embedded&v=HzPSNS3j730.

R-SQUARED

IN EARLY 2012, I received an e-mail from a colleague sharing a URL for a new conference. "Do you know anything about this?" he asked. The Risk and Reward Conference (R2), focusing on creativity and innovation in libraries, was planned for September 2012 up in the mountains in Telluride, Colorado (where the local tourism board won the bid to host the conference).[1] The initial placeholder web page was mysterious, lacking a lot of details one usually finds on conference pages. As more details about R2 appeared in the spring, I was intrigued and decided to attend in spite of relatively high travel and boarding costs, using conference funds made available to me by the provost's office at San José State University.

The Risk and Reward Conference turned out to be a barn burner, and worth the expense. The organizers—from the Colorado State Library, the award-winning Anythink libraries, Wilkinson Public Library in Telluride, and other Colorado institutions—had worked eighteen months on this conference, a quick timeline for such an undertaking. They had put heart and soul into the planning and implementation.

I could tell how important this was to them by tears shed at the conference closing and the incredible attention to detail across the two and half days we spent together: spray-painted conference logos on the streets of Mountain Village, interactive stations around the venue to challenge assumptions and promote creative engagement, and T-shirts displaying the slogan: "'Better safe than sorry' may be the most dangerous thing ever said." I don't think there has ever been a library conference where somebody has stuck their hand into a box that could potentially contain spiders, worms, or snakes as part of the learning.

Over two days we explored creativity and curiosity, heard from keynoters such as Josh Linkner, author of *Disciplined Dreaming,* and each of us chose and completed our own immersive group experience.[2] I chose Customer Curiosity (though other options included Creative Spaces, Culture, and Abundant Community) with John Bellina, from the Denver marketing firm Ricochet Ideas, and Tasso Stathopulos.[3] Ricochet is the design group that helped create Anythink and transformed services such as the Anythink summer reading program through disruptive innovation.[4] Our group worked at turning the conventions and assumptions about Banned Books Week on its ear.[5] Ideas in the form of action briefs flowed (an action brief is a framing statement used in planning that includes who we want to convince about a service or product, how we will do it, and what the service will be that makes the change). Bellina challenged us with, "If we are not offering people something new, are we really doing our jobs?"

This was unlike any library conference I have ever been to, a sentiment echoed by other participants across Twitter, Facebook, and in the hallways of the conference center. What made the difference? I believe that active engagement promotes learning and transformation more than sitting in the room and watching PowerPoint or Keynote slides go by. We were up, we were talking, we were writing and sharing. We were walking around the room answering questions.

BEYOND BEST PRACTICES

It also got me thinking about how many of our conferences in the library world are focused on sharing tips with little context, listening to a track of people tell you how they "did it good" and sharing the best practices for the technology of the day. By contrast, I would call R2 a "conference up on its feet." We were sent out of the conference center looking around the physical world for ideas about how we can make changes to what we do and what we offer.

I would argue that the best practice presentations and technology of the day talks might find a better home via online learning programs and online conferences and events like the Library 2.0 Conference, where participants can listen, learn, and come away with new knowledge from their home base.[6] This would ideally free up our physical conferences to offer more active engagement in the model of R2.

Our profession is ripe for a shake-up in this regard—I think we're getting a little tired of talking heads conference models and the classic format of walking to sessions and sitting for forty-five minutes, lather rinse repeat. I have a hunch that this might explain the uptick of the unconference movement as well.[7] Just taking the pulse of the room via Twitter with the hashtag that we used for the conference (#rsq12), I could tell that people were feeling the same way, that this was something to think about, that this model is one that needs to be propelled forward. Echoed in the halls and at break: "Are you doing it next year? Is this happening again? Are we going to do this again?" R2 should do it again, certainly, but state and national conferences would likewise do well to take a page from this immersive experience program.

OUTSIDE THE ECHO CHAMBER

I also believe that involving those from outside LIS was a key factor to the success of R2.

I love the fact that we had advertising and design thinkers coming in and talking with us: not standing up and telling us what we should do, but actually engaging and answering questions and giving us assignments and then saying come back in twenty minutes with this and we'll talk about it and we'll experience it together.

We're going to look back at this and note that there were conferences before the R2 Conference that were a certain way and conferences that came after R2 became more of this active, on your feet, looking to shake things up and talking with people outside of our field to do so. Writing at Tame the Web, Mace Ojala, a librarian from Finland, echoed my thoughts about his own disruptive experience with the cycling for libraries event: "We need more ways to learn, share, and work together. A lot of new and different ways."[8] I'd add R2 to the list and urge everyone to watch for news of another R2.

My plea to conference organizers: I would like to see more regional conferences in the R2 mold. I want to see more LIS professors and students in attendance, participating as well. It would be wonderful if librarians and LIS folk could have access to meetings like this all over the United States, if not all over the world.

Talking heads and flipping slides will give way to active thinking and challenge-based learning experiences. One of the last things we did as a group at R2 was read aloud a statement prepared by the organizers: "You are not just an employee, volunteer, or board member. You do not merely catalogue books, organize periodicals, and manage resources. You are the gateway into the mind of the idea people who come to our facilities to find or fuel the spark, part wizard, part genius, part explorer. It is your calling to trespass into the unknown and come back with a concrete piece someone can hold on to, turn over, and use to fuel their mind and soul." I kid you not, there were people shedding tears by the end of the reading. It was a beautiful moment.

This conference was not for the faint of heart or the passive "let me sit in my chair and listen and take notes" type. At one point, we were standing on our chairs about to take a great leap of faith (at the behest of a speaker urging us not to wait for three, but to jump on two), looking beyond our fears toward the risks and rewards and the potential for innovation and disruptive service. But once you've done a conference this way, you can never go back.

NOTES

1. Katie Klingsporn, "Risk, Reward and the Survival of Libraries," *Telluride Daily Planet,* September 9, 2011, www.telluridenews.com/news/article_aceda2cd-d604-5f70-83eb-576d0a387a62.html.
2. Josh Linkner, *Disciplined Dreaming: A Proven System to Drive Breakthrough Creativity* (San Francisco: Jossey-Bass, 2011).
3. Ricochet Ideas, www.ricochetideas.com.
4. Anythink Libraries, https://www.anythinklibraries.org.
5. Banned Books Week, www.bannedbooksweek.org.
6. Library 2.0, www.library20.com.
7. "Unconference," *Wikipedia,* https://en.wikipedia.org/wiki/Unconference.
8. Cycling for Libraries, www.cyclingforlibraries.org.

RESEARCHER: WHAT YOU GOT?

A RECENT OPINION piece from Singapore's *Straits Times* recently made the rounds on Facebook. "Prof, No One Is Reading You," by Asit K. Biswas and Julian Kirchherr, explores the idea that most scholarly output disappears into our databases, curriculum vitaes and tenure dossiers, without much readership.[1] "An average academic journal article is read in its entirety by about 10 people," the op-ed piece says, calling for professors to seek exposure of their work in mainstream media. Research, the authors argue, used to sway policy and inform practice across multiple disciplines. Now, not so much.

I'd argue there is definitely a disconnect between LIS professors' scholarly output and the practice of librarianship. Of course, there are some valuable, noteworthy studies—funded by the Institute of Museum and Library Services and other entities—that have influenced libraries and librarianship. But what of the plethora of articles published annually by professors like me, deep in the tenure track, building a record of research? Are they mired behind sites that require payment where no one will see them unless they actively seek them out?

WHAT LEARNERS NEED

Take a look at a recent *Journal of Education for Library and Information Science* (volume 56, no. 2), now an online journal available by subscription and through the usual aggregator databases.[2] I'm struck by the pertinence and usefulness of the articles. For example, take a look at "Competencies for Information Professionals in Learning Labs and Makerspaces," by Kyungwon Koh and June Abbas.[3] Their literature review presents a quick trip through the history of makerspaces and touches on emerging competencies for library staff. Koh and Abbas suggest key competencies needed for successful job performance in learning labs and makerspaces, including the ability to learn, adapt to changing situations, collaborate, advocate for the learning lab or makerspace, and serve diverse people. Their discussion of the findings points to interesting ideas, mapping most of their defined competencies to coordinating competencies from associations such as the Young Adult Library Services Association, American Association of School Librarians, and Association for Library Service to Children. The "ability to learn" and the "ability to adapt to changing situations" are not currently mapped to any competencies promoted by one of our associations. These are rallying cries for our profession.

Koh and Abbas argue, "Knowledge on what users need and how they learn should be a key takeaway for LIS students. The focus of LIS programs needs to be user-centered."[4] Amen. My takeaway is the further revamping of curriculum, away from resources, toward user populations' needs and views. What hiring or strategic planning librarian wouldn't benefit from this study?

PUTTING IT OUT THERE

Dan Savage's *Lovecast* podcast features a segment called "What You Got?" highlighting recent studies from sex and relationship researchers.[5] Savage gives scholars a few minutes of airtime to report on how their findings might relate to listeners. What a brilliant way to get the word out about research! Maybe a similar segment could find its way to Steve Thomas's *Circulating Ideas* podcast, a show I always enjoy.[6]

Conference planners, too, should seek to bridge this divide, inviting academics and practitioners to the same panels and building tracks that allow interested librarians to sample bite-size versions of recent findings. Most Januaries, the Association for Library and Information Science Education meets in the same city as the ALA's Midwinter Meeting. Let's mix it up, spend a day together talking about studies such as the Koh and Abbas piece. I would also recommend that ALA's Midwinter Meeting include a researcher stage (or podium or corner) on the show floor from which researchers could present their work. We should also advocate for more open-access journals that make it easier to tweet, post, and share links to pertinent research.

TELL A STORY

A warning to scholars seeking to cross over: be mindful of writing style. I review manuscripts for a handful of journals and more than once have zoned out trying to make it through a statistics-heavy, stuffy analysis of a research project that could have been made so much more interesting with a story-like narrative that still fits within the academic template. Maybe that's one reason I've always been drawn to qualitative research and its descriptions of experiences and phenomenological explorations. I feel lucky to have been able to weave my own research into my presentations at state associations and elsewhere. I invite LIS scholars to find additional, creative outlets to share their research with a broader audience.

NOTES

1. Asit K. Biswas and Julian Kirchherr, "Prof, No One Is Reading You," *The Straits Times,* April 11, 2015, www.straitstimes.com/opinion/prof-no-one-is-reading-you.
2. *Journal of Education for Library and Information Science,* http://dpi-journals.com/index.php/JELIS/issue/view/144.
3. Kyungwon Koh and June Abbas, "Competencies for Information Professionals in Learning Labs and Makerspaces," *Journal of Education for Library and Information Science* 56, no. 2 (2015): 114–29.
4. Ibid., 124.
5. *Savage Lovecast,* www.savagelovecast.com.
6. *Circulating Ideas,* http://circulatingideas.com.

5

A CURRICULUM FOR LIBRARIANSHIP

Goals, Evolving LIS Curriculum,
Cross-Discipline Collaborations

W HAT GOALS DO we set for an LIS curriculum? Particularly as we implement technological tools into our curriculum, we need to develop a meaningful purpose for their use, such as to prepare LIS students for a decidedly digital future in libraries. The incoming students I've encountered in our program are eager, curious, and excited to learn. This attitude should be encouraged and nurtured through programs and curricula that go beyond the typical and fading models of instruction we so easily rely on. In the pursuit of a better relationship and greater learning, LIS educators must be willing to give up some control and place it in the hands of their capable students. Students have much to contribute; if we continue to teach in the same ways, we limit their potential. Building a well-rounded curriculum around critical thinking and soft skills may involve innovation in our courses and trying out new methods for teaching, like the flipped classroom model.

Sometimes when we use technology in LIS courses, they can become superficial bells and whistles. However, as we specify goals for their use, we can ensure that their main purpose is to build bonds between the educator and student. Creating a participatory culture in our libraries and LIS classes will help place more control in students' hands. It will also prepare students to create a participatory culture in their workplace. These future librarians will also be ready to develop transparent relationships with the communities they serve.

Focusing on collaboration and community involvement will help students keep an appropriate focus on the user even while maintaining stewardship over collections and other library resources. New librarians should come out of LIS programs with technical skills, but also soft skills like communication, initiative, the desire for continuous learning, sensitivity for others, and a keen sense of professional responsibility.

Our LIS educators, while bringing creativity into the classroom, must also remain in touch with what it means to be librarians in the community, on the job. We can do this through continuing education and implementing projects in our classrooms that involve current library issues and concerns. For example, we can put our students in touch with patrons. As LIS students get to know library users, they will better understand how their courses are preparing them to meet users' needs.

LIS professors should be in touch with professional librarians. Library students should be in communication with professors and professionals. The more we open up all channels of conversation, the more transparent our processes and services will become. When we engage in open communication, we create an opportunity for improvement and growth, for greater interconnectedness and community, and for the chance to take librarianship and libraries successfully into the next generation.

GOALS OF AN LIS EDUCATOR

PRESENTING AT THE EDUCAUSE Learning Initiatives (ELI) conference in January 2010 in Austin, Texas, was a seminal moment for me.[1] I found my tribe of like-minded educators and technologists examining what it means to be teaching and creating learning environments in the twenty-first century. What I didn't find was too many librarians; roughly 7 to 8 percent of the 500-plus attendees were librarians. (Note to readers: put this dynamic conference on your radar. More of us should be there to represent and participate in the conversations.)

Beyond the benefits of finding like-minded thinkers, ELI forced me to articulate my personal goals as an LIS educator. One day a tweet went up in the conference back channel: "Digital literacies discussion brings the same concept to the surface each year: Sure, you want to use tech but what's your GOAL?" That tweet sent me back to work on my upcoming presentation about the technologies I was currently using to teach at the Dominican graduate school of library and information science (GSLIS). I spent the night updating my slides to frame what I was doing within a larger context. This exercise helped me clarify my philosophy of LIS education. Some of my goals include the following ones.

To prepare LIS students for a decidedly digital future in libraries. With titles like digital strategy librarian, user experience librarian, or strategy guide, the jobs being advertised speak to an evolving skill set that not only includes a solid understanding of the core values of LIS but a strong knowledge of information architecture, online user behavior, and the ability to build networked resources and services. We do our students (and programs) a disservice if they graduate with only a cursory understanding of library tech—emerging and otherwise.

To remember that twentieth-century policies don't always work in twenty-first-century learning/sharing spaces. As I've already mentioned, I still post library signage on Tame the Web that shows how backward some library policy is. There's just too much competition from other third places for us to greet our user communities with placards proclaiming *No* this and *No* that. Beyond signage, do our user policies extend the library to our constituents in ways that benefit them? Is the library usable?

To promote truth and open communication. For over two years, Michael Casey and I wrote "The Transparent Library" column in *Library Journal*.[2] Transparency—open planning and open communication—should be key in managing our organizations in this post-Web 2.0 world. Institutions bound in secrecy and controlled information flow cannot thrive. New graduates with different mindsets can be change agents—hire them.

To give students environments for exploration and experience. With Dominican GSLIS graduate Kyle Jones, I built online communities for each of my classes. I wanted my students to experience writing on the open web and not behind the firewall of Blackboard. New grads will find few jobs where all of their time will be inside a firewall or hiding in the back of the library. As a service-oriented profession, many of our services have, or will have, an online component. Other jobs and services will take the librarian physically beyond library walls into academic departments or the community.

To immerse students in the spaces and communities where they may work upon graduation. What better place to explore these realms than throughout the curriculum? I applaud the classes I see running in Drupal on the open web or taught via Facebook and Twitter. The tools will change, but the ideas behind them will not. With this comes a chance to reflect on privacy, anonymity, and how best to represent oneself to the professional linked-in world.

To acquaint students with the human connections created by social media. Beyond shiny toys, the tools at our disposal can enhance and augment human relationships. When the technology falls away, we're left with two or more people having a very human conversation. Anyone can write a blog post touting the library's next event; it takes some talent to craft a post that prompts users to respond and share. The more we learn what works to engage and enlighten our communities—virtual and physical—the more we can tap into them.

To help students create their own personal learning network. This is key. Actively participating in various channels that create a learning network—like blogs, Twitter, Facebook group—sets them up to be more connected, to garner interviews and that first professional job. Wouldn't you rather hire someone who understands the ins and outs of the dynamic community of practitioners available to us online—globally?

To learn by doing. The sage on the stage model of lecture no longer flies. Students should explore, play, experiment, and figure things out for themselves. As a teacher, I should serve as a trusty guide, giving them some resources and ideas to spur thinking and set them free. That's the type of learner we want steering our libraries in the future.

These are the goals we should all strive for, to ultimately prepare all learners, patrons, and users for a decidedly digital future.

NOTES

1. EDUCAUSE, www.educause.edu/eli/events/eli-annual-meeting/2010.
2. Michael Stephens, Tame the Web, http://tametheweb.com/2014/03/03/news-download-the-transparent-library-e-book-here/.

OUR COMMON PURPOSE

AN ARTICLE IN the *Chronicle of Higher Education* recounts how Kansas State University professor Michael Wesch "rebooted" his tech-heavy teaching approach after "a frustrated colleague approached him after one of his talks: 'I implemented your idea, and it just didn't work. . . . The students thought it was chaos.'"[1] Instead, Wesch, an associate professor of cultural anthropology, now stresses, "It doesn't matter what method you use if you do not first focus on one intangible factor: the bond between professor and student." Just adding a certain technology to a course will not improve learning or create community. That bond is more important to class success than new technologies, and it has nothing to do with blogs or mobile phones.

The shift was fairly astonishing, since Wesch is the creator of the video *Web 2.0: The Machine Is Us/ing Us*, which has over 11 million views on YouTube, and he has actively used Twitter, YouTube, and other interactive technologies in his classes. [2]

Wesch's advice is just as good for our libraries as for those of us who teach in LIS programs. I emphasize participatory teaching in my classes, a model that shares many commonalities with the library model of participatory service. One aspect of the model is incorporating social media and other emerging technologies into the coursework as a means to "flip" the classroom, so students become active participants and co-collaborators with the professor. But maybe we've gone too far.

FACILITATE NONTECH SKILLS

"Get a blog, launch texting, create a Facebook page" has been the rallying cry—from me, too—for some time, but the reasons for doing these things should be clear. They're an extension of what we have always done, the foundational purpose of libraries. Service. Access. Context.

Many LIS programs include "how-to" technology classes. These are useful for providing the skills new grads need to be marketable. Along with those skill-based courses, however, we must give students opportunities to learn how to engage actively with people, facilitate people's interests and conversation, and promote the creation of community. These concepts should translate from the real world to online and back again.

Peter Block writes in *Community: The Structure of Belonging,* "Communities are human systems given form by conversations that build relatedness."[3] This echoes Wesch's point—building a relationship between the educator and the learner or between the librarian and the user is a step toward establishing the bonds of community. That's why we can't just hide behind our reference desks or our virtual lecterns and hope that students or users listen but leave us alone. Active engagement begins here. If we can articulate our purpose well and use it as a basis for building community, we are on the right track.

Sharing ourselves as educators and librarians should be part of the mix. At a recent all-faculty institute at San José State University, California, professors and adjuncts exchanged tips for developing that sense of relatedness across our virtual program. Posting family photos, communicating within our collaborative instant messaging application, and connecting with students via social media and in-person meet-ups were all among the suggestions.

THINKING OUT LOUD

Wesch also notes that professors trip up by translating traditional methods to these new spaces, like grading blog reflections as though they are finished papers.[4] I recently amended my blogging assignments this semester after reflecting on these ideas and a post by Gardner Campbell, director of professional development and innovative initiatives at Virginia Tech, entitled "Blogs and Baobabs."[5]

I tell my students to think of their blog as a journal intended to help clarify their thoughts while contributing openly on the Web and with the feedback of their classmates, their professor, and possibly the world. My course site says it clearly.

"Important: Let your blogging be a reflection of your own curiosity and ideas about our course. Follow your thoughts where they go. Ponder, for example, how the ideas you are encountering might inform your practice as a librarian or information professional. It is entirely acceptable to 'think aloud' via your blog."

I promise them I will not swoop in and grade down for bad sentence structure or poorly conceived ideas. The blogging space is part of our community of learning each semester and a way to promote connection that also finds its way to Twitter and beyond.

"Only through that sense of connection," states Wesch, "do you have this sense of community."[6] Professors and librarians seeking to convene groups of their constituents might give some thought to establishing a strong bond that doesn't begin and end with the hot technology of the day but something deeper and more meaningful: an understanding of our common purpose.

NOTES

1. Jeffrey R. Young, "A Tech-Happy Professor Reboots after Hearing His Teaching Advice Isn't Working," *The Chronicle of Higher Education*, February, 12, 2012, http://chronicle.com/article/A-Tech-Happy-Professor-Reboots/130741/.
2. YouTube, https://www.youtube.com/watch?v=NLlGopyXT_g.
3. Peter Block, *Community: The Structure of Belonging* (Oakland, CA: Berrett-Koehler, 2009), 33.
4. Young, "A Tech-Happy Professor," http://chronicle.com/article/A-Tech-Happy-Professor-Reboots/130741/.

5. Gardner Campbell, "Blogs and Baobabs," *Gardner Writes: Aut Inveniam, Aut Faciam,* January 16, 2012, www.gardnercampbell.net/blog1/?p=1671.
6. Young, "A Tech-Happy Professor," http://chronicle.com/article/A-Tech-Happy-Professor-Reboots/130741/.

LOST CONTROL? NOT A PROBLEM

IN A DISCUSSION after a recent presentation, an educator stood to make a counterpoint to my take on participatory teaching. "I'm paid to have control," she said. More than one person in the room gasped.

I should have directed her to the 2013 *Horizon Report.* Among the key trends identified as those impacting teaching and learning for 2013 is an emphasis on "open." The report indicates that in the future, education and publication venues will look more and more toward models that provide open access to content.[1]

Open teaching, open courses, open minds. It struck me that emphasizing control over what students read, how they respond to discussion questions, and how, essentially, they learn might not be the best path forward when technology and other trends are rapidly changing the learning landscape. The evolution of trends marked by the *Horizon Report* is fascinating. The 2013 trends include the aforementioned open everything, the significance of informal learning opportunities, socially focused connected learning, and the hurtling locomotive known as MOOCs.[2]

PLAYTIME

I always apply the *Horizon* trends directly to LIS students and the work they will do in various information environments. The *Horizon Report* notes that in addition to formal coursework, "allowing for more open-ended, unstructured time where they are encouraged to experiment, play, and explore topics based on their own motivations" can benefit students and prepare them for the world of work.[3]

I'm reminded of Finland's school system, where an emphasis on "whatever it takes" and play as learning has created one of the best educational systems in the world.[4] Students in the United States are missing out, especially as teaching to the test replaces these key concepts.

In the workplace, I hope new librarians are given a chance to "play" as part of a continuous emphasis on learning. To the commenter who wrote in a letter to *Library Journal* that "none of those who don't have enough time to get the work done have time to 'play,'"[5] I would respectfully disagree. Henry Jenkins defined play as "the capacity to experiment with one's surroundings as a form of problem-solving."[6] Isn't that the type of librarian we want as colleagues? Problem-solvers who can find solutions by active consideration of the issue? To me, that's a significant component of "learning to learn."

FLIPPING OUT

A key trend that came from the 2012 *Horizon Report*—"The abundance of resources and relationships made easily accessible via the Internet is increasingly challenging us to revisit our roles as educators"—speaks directly to the open versus control debate above.[7] I would advocate flipping everything we can in LIS education. *Flipping* is defined as inverting norms within education. Flipped classrooms might come in the form of open social spaces where students can learn, reflect, and interact with practitioners. Flipped resources might occur in the form of open-source textbooks that grow and evolve as quickly as ideas and trends do. How much longer is it feasible and useful to require students to purchase books that cost $60 or more when these static tomes collide with the potential of open-access articles, chapters, and interactive content?

MASSIVELY COOL

A buzz-worthy, hot topic of the day is that the MOOC brings these ideas together. An arena of connected, open learning—offered for free—has the potential to impact not only higher education but library services as well. How will we support students of all kinds in MOOCs? What happens to the potential for professional development and lifelong learning when courses can gather the best of the best in a field and offer experiences and exploration anywhere? What barriers need to fall in our institutions to promote these opportunities?

In these spaces, control flips as well. Guess what, educator—you are no longer in charge of your realm! Giving students control recognizes them as active contributors to the learning process, engages them in a way in which they're accustomed to operating, and is built on mutual respect.

Consider the future of the hyperlinked library. It might be a little less structured than that to which we are accustomed. It might be messy at times. But there's synchronicity in some of the themes I've discussed—chaos, participatory culture, learning everywhere—and the trends identified in the *Horizon Report*. The shifts noted above will surely impact not only LIS education but all libraries that support learning. Losing a bit of control opens the heart and the mind to what the future will bring.

NOTES

1. Larry Johnson, S. Adams Becker, M. Cummins, V. Estrada, A. Freeman, and H. Ludgate, *NMC Horizon Report: 2013 Higher Education Edition* (Austin, TX: New Media Consortium, 2013), www.nmc.org/pdf/2013-horizon-report-HE.pdf.
2. Ibid., 7.
3. Ibid.
4. LynNell Hancock, "Why Are Finland's Schools Successful?" *Smithsonian Magazine,* September 2011, www.smithsonianmag.com/innovation/why-are-finlands-schools-successful-49859555/?no-ist=.
5. Name Withheld Upon Request, "What About Our Work," *Library Journal,* February 4, 2013, http://lj.libraryjournal.com/2013/02/opinion/feedback-letters-to-lj-february-1-2013-issue/#_.
6. Henry Jenkins, "Confronting the Challenges of Participatory Culture: Media Education of the 21st Century," *National Writing Project,* 2006, www.nwp.org/cs/public/print/resource/2713.
7. Larry Johnson, S. Adams, and M. Cummins, *NMC Horizon Report: 2012 Higher Education Edition* (Austin, TX: New Media Consortium, 2012), 4, www.nmc.org/pdf/2012-horizon-report-HE.pdf.

COLLECTION BASHING AND TRASHING

I'VE SAID BEFORE that one of the things preventing librarians from working at web scale might be "a lingering emphasis on collections over users." Others and I have argued that the evolution of libraries and library service will include a pronounced shift from libraries as book warehouses to libraries as centers for discovery, learning, and creation via any number of platforms.

I might have been guilty of a bit of collection bashing in these discussions, and recent occurrences of collection trashing have given me pause. I still see the path forward detailed above as viable and inevitable, but we should not forget that stewardship must not be sacrificed for a 3-D printer or a wall of monitors highlighting a digital collection.

LEARNING FROM #BOOKGATE

I followed with great interest the weeding kerfuffle now known as #bookgate at the Urbana Free Library (UFL) in Illinois.[1] Tweets, news stories, and Facebook shares painted a grim picture of a weeding project gone horribly wrong. In a nutshell: books more than ten years old were removed from the nonfiction collection without reference to any other criteria.

I wished Michael Casey (now information technology director, Gwinnett County Public Library, Georgia) and I were still writing *Library Journal*'s "Transparent Library" column, because as the story unfolded, most of what I read about the weeding process and administration of UFL was decidedly opaque.[2] A possibly misguided strategic planning process was criticized as lacking community involvement.

Outrage ensued across the online spaces librarians inhabit, as well as those of UFL patrons and watchdog types. I would call this an example of closed governance—something we see going away, quickly, in the face of the open government movement. It will also be a case study to end all case studies in collection development and management classes across LIS.

Carol Tilley, assistant professor at the graduate school of library and information science, University of Illinois at Urbana-Champaign, was instrumental in sharing links, commentary, and retweets during #bookgate and, with others in the community, put together a website devoted to reclaiming and supporting UFL.[3] It will remain a valuable resource even after the immediate crisis is resolved, because all of us in the field should learn from these events.

Even as books go digital and directly to readers' devices, there are still print materials and media to purchase and share—and de-select when the time comes and criteria are met. Engaging with the public during each step of this process keeps them involved and reduces after-the-fact wrath.

One of Tilley's Twitter shares was about the Onondaga Public Library in Syracuse, New York, publicizing their campaign to save 1,100 vintage science fiction books from destruction.[4] The library sought creative proposals for passing on a little-used science fiction collection. Great books, not circulating, must go to good homes, the library was essentially saying. That's transparency at its best—transparent and shared leadership. Organizations like libraries can either battle their public or work with it. The long-term solution is openness.

BEYOND THE COLLECTION

The tale of #bookgate should be a catalyst for librarians to offer more participatory avenues, to engage with not only the care and nurturing of our collections but with all aspects of our services. A library operating without the input of its constituents is missing a vital component.

I bounced these thoughts off Casey, who replied, "We can even look to radically transparent movements in the area of government budget-building with some of the new participatory budgeting processes coming out of Chicago and New York City. Urbana and some other libraries would do well to look to some newer forms of radical transparency."

Programming is another area where public involvement would enhance offerings. Does your library engage with a group of constituents to map out possible ideas for programs and events? Are you still offering the same programs you developed years ago because they are easy to replicate? Paying attention to user interests will help gauge what's hot right now. Fresh voices and ideas from beyond library staff input might lead to some intriguing and popular initiatives.

These ideas should also permeate our work in LIS classrooms. LIS courses that incorporate participatory design into student work give new graduates the skills and mind-set to use it in practice. One summer, my co-instructor, Kyle Jones, and I designed a new assignment for the hyperlinked library MOOC that my school offers.[5] This community engagement exercise gets our students thinking about building services and planning for the future with participation and feedback from all stakeholders. I hope libraries considering sweeping changes will do the same.

NOTES

1. Urbana Free Library, http://urbanafreelibrary.org/search/node/bookgate.
2. *Library Journal*, http://lj.libraryjournal.com/2007/06/future-of-libraries/the-transparent-library-living-out-loud/#_.
3. Reclaiming Our Library, http://reclaimingourlibrary.blogspot.com/2013/07/a-few-reasons-you-should-care-about.html.
4. "Save 1,100 Vintage Science Fiction Books from Destruction!" http://io9.gizmodo.com/save-1-100-vintage-science-fiction-books-from-destructi-752523735.
5. San José State University, http://ischool.sjsu.edu/programs/moocs/hyperlinked-library-mooc.

ESSENTIAL SOFT SKILLS

ARE WE PREPARING graduates for the information workplace? That's a question I considered when I first read Paul Fain's article, "Grading Personal Responsibility," from *Inside Higher Ed*.[1] He describes a new initiative at Asheville-Buncombe Technical Community College, North Carolina, emphasizing "soft skills" as part of the curriculum, including personal responsibility, interdependence, and emotional intelligence.

These are important concepts to consider, and I wonder just how much emphasis is placed on these types of skills as students move through our programs. Are LIS graduates as work-ready as they could be? Are there some soft skills particularly necessary in information professions? Consider the following soft skills essential for our libraries and information centers.

COMMUNICATION

A given, right? It should be a tremendous concern if a student is graduating without experience communicating via the written word, as a participant in a conversation or group meeting, as a presenter in front of groups, and online within various interactive channels. Clear, concise writing no matter what the format—memo, proposal, brief, e-mail, blog post, Facebook post, tweet—is paramount. A focus on literacy, in every sense of the word, should be crucial as students move toward their degree.

INITIATIVE

I would also stress the willingness to speak up and be heard. New librarians are often too silent. Of course, they shouldn't be annoying or act as know-it-alls—those traits are career killers—but they should be willing to submit ideas up the chain, talk to higher-level administrators when they can, and use their communication skills to make themselves heard, recognized, and appreciated. They should join teams, even during probationary periods, and submit ideas for efficiencies and improvements. With money tight and staff limited, any good administrator is going to welcome this type of new librarian.

We don't have the luxury to have new hires wait for detailed step-by-step assignments or direction. Librarians should take their projects and run with them and have the support of their administration to do so. Is the student who asks multiple questions about every detail of an assignment destined to be the hesitant micromanager hooked on having meetings with little tangible outcomes?

CONTINUOUS LEARNING

I can't emphasize this enough. New hires should have a personal learning environment that is constantly refined and updated as interests shift and emerging trends impact information work. I advocate for interviewers to include, "Describe your personal learning network—how do you continuously learn?" in their list of questions for potential hires. Of course, libraries will provide opportunities for professional development, but this kind of growth starts with the individual.

SENSITIVITY AND UNDERSTANDING

You must be a people person in today's library. Empathic listening goes hand in hand with acceptance. This may be one of the hardest skills to teach and to measure, but a focus on service learning, with "in the field" experience, may provide much-needed guidance in this direction.

PROFESSIONAL RESPONSIBILITY

This skill is threefold. We must be true to ourselves, true to our employers, and true to the ethics and tenets of the profession. A recent study by the Society for Human Resource Management and the AARP cited in the *Wall Street Journal* found "that 'professionalism' or 'work ethic' is the top 'applied' skill that younger workers lack."[2] I tell my students to establish their own professional mission statement or guiding philosophy, to rise above negativity they encounter in the workplace and in our field, and to always remember they are role models for the professionals that will come after them.

FURTHER SKILLS

I would add other soft skills such as intuition, political awareness, and a willingness to make and learn from our mistakes. Transparency is evolving into an even more clearly defined "full frontal" strategy for some corporations—putting it all out there. We should follow suit. Library schools should teach case studies of failed library systems and initiatives. We must study our failures as much as we study our successes. There seems to be an ongoing unwillingness to do this. But in fact some libraries make bad decisions, and we have to admit that in order to learn those corrective lessons.

What soft skills would you add? What traits are needed for twenty-first-century information work? The crux of the matter is this: these skills should be taught throughout our programs, from core courses to electives, practicums, and culminating experiences. Teachers should not only teach these skills, they should model them. It's a tall order for our evolving curriculum, and assessing skills such as intuition and sensitivity is tough. The yield of such hard work, however, is an evolved institution that trains dynamic, responsive library professionals.

NOTES

1. Paul Fain, "Grading Personal Responsibility," *Inside Higher Ed,* December 13, 2012, https://www.insidehighered.com/news/2012/12/13/nc-community-college-issue-grades-certificates-soft-skills.
2. Nick Schulz, "Hard Unemployment Truths about 'Soft' Skills," *The Wall Street Journal,* September 29, 2012, www.wsj.com/articles/SB10000872396390444517 304577653383308386956.

CITATION FIXATION

A WHILE AGO I visited Limerick, Ireland, where I spoke at the International Federation of Library Associations and Institutions' (IFLA) Information Literacy Satellite Conference before heading to Lyon, France, for IFLA proper. The conversations and presentations were thought-provoking, focused on the constantly evolving definition and approaches for teaching information literacy. Why aren't students good writers? What prevents them from doing their best work? Are devices to blame? Short attention spans? Rock and roll?

An odd thought bubbled up: Are we sometimes too concerned about process and what we think students are doing wrong that we miss what they are doing right? To put a fine point on it, are we too hung up on proper citation formatting?

I call this "citation fixation," and when I asked my colleague—Michelle Simmons—for her take, she shared a handout with me that she gives her students each semester. In it, Simmons notes, "Remember that the purpose of a citation is to help your reader find the source, so give enough information that I'll be able to find the source if I want to. Then let it go."

LET IT GO

Michelle cites a blog post from Barbara Fister at ACRLog. "Manual Labor" decries some of the changes and turmoil associated with the various style manuals and gets to the core concern I have: "What exactly are the learning outcomes of creating an error-free list of references?"[1] That made me immediately run to my rubrics to make sure I wasn't focusing too much on the minutiae of citation. No, I just had a note to use a consistent style.

Kurt Schick at the *Chronicle of Higher Education* calls the issue at hand "Citation Obsession" and writes, "nitpicky professors hinder student writers' development by effectively forcing them to invest more time and thinking in less important elements of writing."[2]

But wait—shouldn't we be teaching soon-to-be librarians how to cite properly so they in turn can deliver the gospel to their young charges in the university? And grading them down for every missed period or italicized article title? I'd argue that instead of citation fixation we promote reflection and consideration of the ideas presented in our courses. *To synthesize* is a sometimes overused verb in higher education, but it works in this instance. Students encountering new ideas and voices of any discipline are better served by someone who can nudge them toward critical examination and combining ideas into cohesive structures that help them understand the world. From that understanding should come new ideas, not a perfectly cited reference.

Conor Galvin, director of graduate studies at the University College Dublin (UCD) College of Human Sciences, spoke to these ideas at the IFLA pre-conference. He emphasized the need for librarians to focus on mentoring students and encouraging them while they make their own way through the research process. "It's the difference between learning stuff one-off and learning how to think," he said.

So what are we missing when the focus lands on correct citation style and not the content students are creating? It might be hidden diamonds in the rough, ideas that, with thoughtful critique and revision, could truly shine. See the citation project for some recent research concerning student writing skills.[3]

RISE OF THE MACHINES

So why so many formats? Why so complicated? And why, in the year 2016, are students still creating them instead of machines? Let the machines do the work. Citation managers, although not perfect, can lighten the load of citing multiple types of sources. They need to improve, however. The librarian who invents a working, always correct citation style generator should get a prize. The educators who pull back from an overemphasis on correct citations also should get an award. And to the brilliant person who conceives a better way to point readers to sources that cuts through all the confusion, proprietary voodoo, and punctuation mumbo jumbo—kudos!

HYPERLINKED WORLD

Citations are hyperlinks, right? Maybe it would be best to direct the user to the source. That's all. Every article, every book, and, of course, every website should have a simple hyperlink. (Creating such a system will require reparations of extensive link rot and more. Taking an example from the work of the International DOI Foundation might be a welcome step.) If it's not online, like many books, why not just use the ISBN? Citations as we use them are leftovers from the pre-computer era.

What we need to do is develop an accepted, easy-to-use format that is as simple as possible. (One example of such simplicity is Apple University's presentation on Picasso's Bull, which is progressively stripped down to its essentials.)[4] Focusing on complex citations—or MARC records or shelving systems—may allow for more precision but at the cost of turning people off. It isn't worth it.

NOTES

1. Barbara Fister, "Manual Labor," *ACRLog*, October 18, 2009, http://acrlog. org/2009/10/18/manual-labor/.
2. Kurt Schick, "Citation Obsession? Get Over It!" *The Chronicle of Higher Education*, October 30, 2011, http://chronicle.com/article/Citation-Obsession-Get-Over/129575/.
3. Citation Project, http://site.citationproject.net.
4. Ben Fox Rubin, "Apple University Preaches Mantra of Simplicity to Employees," *CNET*, August 11, 2014, www.cnet.com/news/apple-university-preaches-mantra-of-simplicity-to-employees/.

FLIPPING THE LIS CLASSROOM

PREVIOUSLY, I WROTE about the San José State University's School of Library and Information Science's (SLIS) evaluation of its core courses.[1] Through this, we reimagined our 200 class titled "Information Communities." While colleagues reworked other core courses, I partnered with Debra Hansen, one of our senior faculty and a library historian, to create an evolving, modern course that presents students with our foundations as well as an overview of information users and the social, cultural, economic, technological, and political forces that shape their information access.

We worked hard to align our new course with some of the most recent discourse concerning teaching and learning. The 2014 *Horizon Report* lists flipped classrooms as an important development in education impacting within one year or less.[2] The flipped model features lecture-style content consumed before class so that class time can be spent more collaboratively. In our 100 percent online model at SLIS, this means we have gathered experts to record a series of lectures on the various module topics. This frees instructors to focus on the more participatory aspects of the course: commenting on student blogs, forums, social media, and one-on-one interaction with students. From the vernacular of MOOCs comes the concept of wrappers, where faculty use prepared core content and "wrap" their own lectures, readings, and insight around it. Our instructors will personalize each module to reflect their own information communities. It is a great concept for a team-taught class. Students benefit from the expertise of a group of instructors, not just one.

LOOKING OUT

Framing the course as outward-facing resonates strongly with me because it reflects exactly how our graduates and information professionals should view the world. Instead of putting the library in the center, we've placed the user there. To quote Karen Schneider, "the user is the sun."[3] From *The Encyclopedia of Community,* Joan Durrance and Karen Fisher's definitive entry provided a theoretical framework: information communities promote a common interest around the creation and exchange of distributed information, may be built around different focal points and topics, can emerge and function without geographical boundaries, and often exploit the Internet and technology.[4] Each module explores these ideas and weaves in ways that libraries and information organizations can support diverse communities of information seekers, users, and creators.

Shades of Seth Godin's *Tribes* and Clay Shirky's *Here Comes Everybody* color this approach and set students on a path to enter the profession understanding that community needs and service should come first.[5] A healthy dose of Henry Jenkins's *Participatory Culture* rounds out the mix.[6] Community members aren't just consuming information; they are generating new knowledge and new ideas.

TUNING IN

Hansen and I received a grant from the Textbook Alternatives Project and Affordable Learning Solutions at the SJSU King Library to develop a course text of library and open-access readings, sparing students the purchase of an expensive, commercially published tome. How liberating it was to mine recent open-access scholarly works, web-published reports, and the wealth of professional literature online via our library to build our text. The module resources and lectures will evolve via new additions and deletions. Just like a library mission statement or technology plan, these aspects of the course should be "living and breathing," not frozen in time.

TURNING ON

I'm most excited about the requirement for student reflection blogging in this course. Discussion forums, landlocked inside the learning management system, are giving way to a WordPress-enabled blog community that all of our core students will work with for thoughts on the course content. I am a longtime advocate of the power of blogging as a means to foster critical reflection in a safe thinking-out-loud space and promote engagement with other students and faculty via commenting. The Online Learning Consortium, devoted to effective online education, recently heralded a similar model: the University of Nevada Las Vegas Journalism School's use of WordPress and BuddyPress for multiuser blogging was cited as an educational innovation.[7]

Additionally, blogging in an open community will give our students experience conducting themselves professionally online from the get-go. It's never too early to learn how to participate constructively.

How does this approach positively impact the profession? I'd argue that students who experience a flipped environment will be better equipped to interact with, collaborate with, and teach others in their communities.

NOTES

1. Michael Stephens, "An Evolving LIS Core," *Library Journal: Office Hours,* November 21, 2012, http://lj.libraryjournal.com/2012/11/opinion/michael-stephens/an-evolving-lis-core-office-hours/#_.
2. Larry Johnson, S. Adams Becker, V. Estrada, and A. Freeman, *NMC Horizon Report: 2014 Higher Education Edition* (Austin, TX: New Media Consortium, 2014), 36, www.nmc.org/pdf/2014-nmc-horizon-report-he-EN.pdf.

3. Karen Schneider, "The User Is Not Broken: A Meme Masquerading as a Manifesto," *Free Range Librarian,* June 3, 2006, http://freerangelibrarian. com/2006/06/03/the-user-is-not-broken-a-meme-masquerading-as-a-manifesto/.
4. Karen E. Fisher and Joan C. Durrance, "Information Communities," in *Encyclopedia of Community: From the Village to the Virtual World,* ed. Karen Christensen and David Levinson (Thousand Oaks, CA: Sage, 2003), 659.
5. Seth Godin, *Tribes: We Need You to Lead Us* (New York: Portfolio, 2008); Clay Shirky, *Here Comes Everybody: The Power of Organizing without Organizations* (New York: Penguin, 2008).
6. Henry Jenkins, *Confronting the Challenges of Participatory Culture: Media Education for the 21st Century* (Cambridge, MA: MIT Press, 2009).
7. Michael Wilder, "Multiuser Blogging as an Educational Innovation," *Online Learning Consortium,* 2013, http://olc.onlinelearningconsortium.org/effective_ practices/multiuser-blogging-educational-innovation.

BRIDGING THE LIS/LIBRARY DIVIDE

IT'S A SONG you may have heard before. Are the majority of educators out of touch with the realities of the professions they support, including those in LIS? How do we prepare our students for a rapidly changing field?

Scott Walter, university librarian at DePaul University, Chicago, once tagged me in a Facebook post pointing to an article from *Inside Higher Ed* titled "The J-School Bubble."[1] Highlighting a Poynter study, the article notes that "96 percent of journalism educators believe that a journalism degree is very important or extremely important when it comes to understanding the value of journalism," while "57 percent of media professionals believe that a journalism degree is key to understanding the value of their field."

Howard Finberg, the author of the journalism study, shares two "big takeaways."[2] For the academics, he believes, "journalism educators should start experimenting and innovating and using digital tools and more innovative teaching methods." Current journalism school students and professionals, he notes, "have a stake in their education, and they need to raise their voices as to what they want and need to see in [journalism programs]."

WHAT ABOUT LIS?

I share Walter's question posted with the link: what would the same study show in LIS education? My answer, after some consideration: the results would probably be similar on both sides. But maybe the deck is stacked. Of course professors and those teaching in LIS programs would maintain that the degree is valuable and necessary. Professors want job security, too. Those in the field—hiring librarians and administrators—might not feel as strongly about the professional credential, and doesn't it seem that those in practice might feel that their education hadn't prepared them for the realities of the work they do? Google "what I didn't learn in library school" for further insight.

Still, I would argue that our field is not quite in the same position as journalism. The impact of the Internet may have moved the newspaper industry toward extinction, but I see many librarians evolving with the sweeping socio-technical changes brought on by the Web.

I'd also argue that the benefits of the study above are in the takeaways Finberg identifies. Yet, these too seem familiar. Of course we want LIS educators who are innovative and cutting edge, flipping their classrooms, responding quickly to changes in library services, and moving to collaborative, project-based learning. But we also want LIS students who take control of and responsibility for their education.

BEEF UP CE

Other professions (though not journalism) have strict continuing education (CE) requirements. CE, mostly carried out by consortia and state or national associations, is not as formalized for us. Consider this another call for professional development "with teeth." Professional librarians should be expected to be always adding skills and knowledge as part of their duties. Formalizing a rigorous process says we mean business. Wafting through a few conference sessions, sitting with a group for a webinar over the lunch hour, or spending a desk shift doing "professional reading" should yield to more active and transparent forms of learning. Could MOOCs for CE be an avenue to explore?

Other actions might address the divide between educators and those in practice or those studying to join the field. LIS professors should follow Finberg's advice above but also actively engage with those in practice on an ongoing basis to ensure their teaching areas are current and aligned with changes in the field. I've long advocated for librarians to be visible to their constituents, but the same goes for LIS educators. The Part-Time Faculty Special Interest Group in the Association for Library and Information Science Education (which could encompass a large number of working professionals) and the LIS Education Discussion Group in the Association of College and Research Libraries are examples of opportunities for conversation.[3] If you're on the advisory board of a library school, be sure to participate in the conversation, ask the difficult questions, and request follow-through and reports for strategic and curricular initiatives.

Recently, I worked on disseminating the Salzburg Curriculum, a document created at the Salzburg Global Seminar during an event cosponsored by the Institute of Museum and Library Services, "Libraries and Museums in an Era of Participatory Culture."[4] We're launching a website for LIS educators and practitioners to review the curriculum and share ideas related to its implementation in library and museum education. Please join the conversation.

I would like to see a study of this caliber replicated in our profession. Survey responses and qualitative data from open-ended questions might be powerful and persuasive for guiding future changes to our professional degree. Bridging that divide may be a key factor in the evolution of library education.

NOTES

1. Colleen Flaherty, "The J-School Bubble," *Inside Higher Ed*, August 9, 2013, https://www.insidehighered.com/news/2013/08/09/study-points-gaps-between-how-journalism-educators-and-journalists-view-j-schools.
2. Ibid.
3. Association for Library and Information Science Education, http://aliseparttimeadjunctsfacultysig.weebly.com; Association of College and Research Libraries, www.ala.org/acrl/aboutacrl/directoryofleadership/interestgroups/acr-iglise.
4. Salzburg Curriculum, http://salzburg.hyperlib.sjsu.edu.

LISTENING TO STUDENT VOICES

HOWEVER ENGAGING, THOUGHT-PROVOKING, and even polarizing the speakers were at the Future of Academic Libraries Symposium presented by McMaster University and *Library Journal,* they couldn't match what five McMaster University students had to say.[1] "Hearing from Our Users: What Students Expect," moderated by Mike Ridley, who at the time was chief librarian and information officer at the University of Guelph, offered the most striking, honest, and emotionally charged views of the entire day. It gave symposium participants a glimpse of students' perceptions and opinions.

Ridley urged the panel to "tell us what we need to hear," and they did.[2] While all five own a smartphone, not one said they had ever accessed library resources on their device, although all were involved in extracurricular activities, had part-time jobs, and volunteered their time. Comments from the panel were telling, humorous ("the food at the library sucks"), and eye-opening ("we need more one-on-one interaction with the librarians"), offering much to ponder. Some of the takeaways that resonated for me should directly impact the LIS curriculum.

WHAT THEY SAID

Our stuff is hard to use and not very simple to navigate for answers or resources. "Why do so many of you start with Google?" Ridley asked.[3] One concise answer spoke volumes to the crowd: "Efficiency and accessibility—the simplicity. The library website is hard to use. You should not have to teach us how to use the [web]site—it should be obvious." A student who is very fond of books always starts her research in the stacks. "It's hard to figure out what database to use and that's where the disconnect is," she said.

WHAT WE SHOULD DO

Information architecture, usability, and emphasis on user experience and design should be included in every LIS student's program.

It's hard to imagine a professional position that might not include creating content, designing web services for users, or performing some form of instruction related to the site. If a site is difficult to navigate, will students ever want to return to it when the simplicity and "just in time" allure of Google calls?

WHAT THEY SAID

One of the panelists reported he had been unaware of most library services until he took a course in library use.[4] "We're going to teach you to search . . . ," the librarian said in class, and he responded with a big "eye roll." He soon realized how useful that knowledge could be.

Students don't want noisy messages from the library; they're a problem. Be in the social spaces, the panelists urged, but "don't flood us with the same old stuff you always send."

WHAT WE SHOULD DO

Marketing and creating a presence that reaches out to students are just as important as having usable sites. Many LIS students take a user instruction course, but they need a broader view on how to interact with student users via various channels. Such instruction might provide more insight into student behavior as well as tactics for getting the message out about what's available at the library. As I've said before, we need to move from source-focused to research process-focused instruction. And we should find ways to do it at the point of need for students because many are not coming to ask the librarians waiting for them in the library.

WHAT THEY SAID

The age-old confusion about what a librarian does still exists. In fact, when Ridley asked the panel "What defines a professional librarian," their comments weren't surprising.[5] One "had no idea" what a librarian was until it was explained to her in the car on the way to the symposium. Another stated what many students, and public library patrons, think as well: "It means everyone in the library to me." Ridley followed with, "Do you care if it's a librarian, or not, helping you with your research?" The consensus was a simple "No, we just want help," and frankly librarians are mostly a "last resort."

MORE DIFFICULT TRUTHS

One panelist asked that librarians "focus on things we want to talk about," not just on how to search.[6] This goes beyond designing sites and services to something deeper—that human connection forged when we understand each other. How can we reach students, how can we have a tangible impact on their education and their lives, when the disconnect with these articulate, thoughtful young people is so pronounced?

One audience member questioned the group: were they typical students or high achievers?[7] The panelists agreed they were typical—but even if that's not the case, it shouldn't devalue their opinions or any of the opinions our constituents have. We need to hear, understand, and respond to all of these voices. We need a higher level of engagement and understanding of all our users—students, faculty, people.

NOTES

1. YouTube, https://www.youtube.com/watch?v=tzXsd-h-xMs.
2. Ibid.
3. Ibid.
4. Ibid.
5. Ibid.
6. Ibid.
7. Ibid.

THE TRANSPARENT LIBRARY SCHOOL

LIS FACULTY, ADMINISTRATORS, and other stakeholders could take a lesson in transparency from their students. At the "Hack Library School" blog, students in various LIS programs around the country offer up opinions, insights, and some useful truths about their LIS education.[1] Past posts have compared information architecture courses across schools and addressed the divide in classes between students whose focus is user services and those focused on technical services.

The posts are open, straightforward, and reflective. The discourse is transparent.

Individual student blogs like Ben Lainhart's also offer a glimpse into the detailed workings of LIS coursework. In his "Is Online Education Still Stuck in 2001?" he writes about taking an online course that featured an out-of-date textbook as well as a less than engaging delivery: "I do not want to take any more online classes that are exactly the same: sign into [Blackboard], read the 'lecture,' read the articles, make my obligatory posts on the discussion board and occasionally write a paper. How uninspiring!"[2] Later in his post, Lainhart adds, "I am convinced that there have been days that I have learned more on Twitter than from an entire class."

HERE COMES EVERYONE

Education should be inspiring for all involved. Learning should be filled with discovery, encouragement, and experimentation—both with ideas and tools. The best online and in-classroom experiences can and should be enhanced by the online LIS professional commons.

Apparently, some LIS schools need a big dose of radical transparency. The issues and ideas relating to openness and communication in libraries that Michael Casey and I explored in *Library Journal* in "The Transparent Library" column apply equally to LIS education.[3] Library school students deserve a less opaque educational environment, too.

From admission to graduation and beyond, students should be encouraged to engage with faculty and administration in open forums about everything related to their programs: coursework, curriculum, accreditation standards, long-range planning, and faculty hires. School committees made up of all stakeholders should post their minutes and plans to the Web for comments and sharing.

THE BIG PICTURE

Course evaluations alone are not enough. We need ongoing "big picture" program evaluations presenting students and others with a chance to weigh in on issues beyond individual classes and professors. Schedules of courses, environments for learning (even "the classroom was always freezing!"), and information technology infrastructure might be some of the issues ripe for feedback. Appropriate administrators would be expected to respond openly, with the opportunity for further sharing and conversation.

Students would benefit from coauthoring or co-creating class resources with faculty. For many courses, a stale textbook might give way to a collection of web resources, online articles, and the voices of practitioners shared via social media.

The curriculum itself should be nimble and easily adaptable to changes in the profession and technology. One seminar section a semester might focus on bleeding-edge ideas or trends and how libraries might respond to them. Professors might guide the group, but students would be on equal footing to present information and perceptions.

Imagine a seminar on local community support-building, or one on dealing with budget problems on a local level where students hear from some of the key players and get to discuss possible solutions in a more real-world environment and not isolated in a classroom. Transparent discussions in practical decision-making would be invaluable.

GLOBAL SHARING

Beyond these mainly internal changes focusing individual schools outward, the next step is to take the conversation global. I'd like to see a community site like "Hack Library School" include students, professors, deans, and others, plus those who will be hiring new grads. Here's where an organization such as the Association for Library and Information Science Education might play a role, as might library schools and associations from other parts of the world.

With such transparency also comes radical trust. Yes, anonymous comments might encourage a negative, slam book "Rate My Professor"-style environment on the school blog, but most students given the chance to engage would do so positively and with respect.

Just like libraries, the transparent library school needs only to create guidelines for the use of communication tools. Fear of open communication or too much emphasis on command and control does not create the encouraging environment needed to foster twenty-first-century information professionals.

NOTES

1. *Hack Library School*, http://hacklibraryschool.com.
2. Ben Lainhart, "Is Online Education Still Stuck in 2001?" cited at http://tametheweb.com/2011/04/11/office-hours-extra-is-online-education-still-stuck-in-2001/.
3. "The Transparent Library," *Library Journal*, http://lj.libraryjournal.com/2007/04/ljarchives/the-transparent-library-introducing-the-michaels/.

6

INFINITE LEARNING

*Library Learning, Collaboration, Support,
Professional Development*

IN OUR TECHNOLOGY-DRIVEN world, libraries need to take a leadership role in changing learning environments. "Learning in the warehouse"—that solitary library activity of finding a needed book and reading it quietly—has given way to collaborative spaces that facilitate lifelong learning and help our communities develop literacies that are necessary for successful functioning in today's society. Emerging technologies can change our library services and library learning. We can enhance place-based services as well as mobile opportunities for learning, reaching our patrons wherever they are. We can do this with courses too, freeing up time to build more active learning experiences.

When we are in our physical library spaces or on campus for classes, we must focus on innovative pedagogical practices, creating creative learning environments for students and patrons alike. If we want to build these creative spaces, if we want to meet every patron need, we might need to look beyond ourselves and bring in staff who have additional areas of expertise to augment our knowledgeable personnel further. It's not unheard of for librarians to work alongside instructional designers, information architects, and user experience specialists in this new landscape of learning.

Fortunately, library services and practices and skill sets have been evolving for many years as we hone our craft and learn continuously via various platforms. We will continue to adapt and become what our patrons need, molding our physical and online spaces accordingly. There will always be room to grow.

INFINITE LEARNING

DEEP IN THE conversations streams of the Hyperlinked Library MOOC, the large-scale professional development course I have co-taught for more than three hundred library folk, my thoughts turn again to the concept of librarians as facilitators of learning. It becomes clear to me that as learning goes on the move, we not only must keep up with significant changes in education environments but aim to become connectors and collaborators within our users' learning spaces.

FUTURE THINKING

Imagine these scenarios:

A collective of educators and librarians align to offer an online learning program fashioned on the Learning 2.0 model but aimed at enhancing the public's digital literacies, those skills everyone needs to live and work in our hyperconnected world. The authors of an Institute of Museum and Library Services report entitled "Building Digital Communities" define digital literacy as the "effective use of information and communication technologies."[1] I might call them "life literacies." Without access to these skills, the report states, "full participation in nearly every aspect of American society—from economic success and educational achievement, to positive health outcomes and civic engagement—is compromised."[2] Lifelong learning goes hand in hand with life literacy.

A public library offers its patrons online courses with content from the community's experts. Partnerships are formed. Localized learning and collaboration play out between a socially focused course platform and in-person meet-ups hosted at the library and around town. Library staff facilitate the course, helping not only to create connections but to assist participants with the creation of deliverables. I've seen the seeds of this at Library You, the clearing-house from the Escondido Public Library, California, which collects and shares local knowledge through videos and podcasts.[3] On the academic side, the University of British Columbia (UBC) is offering a new LOOC—local open online course—open to anyone with a campus-wide UBC login ID.[4]

Amid the day-to-day work of assisting students, coordinating purchase of online resources, and planning for future collaborative spaces, a university librarian is called upon to assist a professor with her "flipped classroom" online.

IN THE NOW

That last item wasn't future dreaming, but recently featured in a post by Brian Mathews at the *Chronicle of Higher Education*.[5] Mathews opines that curating the learning experience may be something many librarians may soon support. "Personalized virtual communities for teaching and research are primed to be one of the next big things for librarians and academia," he writes. "It's part of the transition we face from content providers to engagement developers." I'm with you, Brian, and I appreciate your carefully chosen words to define these new roles: "learning experience curator" and "engagement developer" may sound buzzwordy, but they describe some significant alterations to our skill sets.

Public libraries are the best platforms for success with community-focused online learning of all sizes. It's easy to create successful MOOCs in an academic environment. It's something else to make them successful in a nonacademic environment. Jeff Jarvis, on *This Week in Google,* discussed the idea of unbundling education from universities, unbundling lessons from courses, and looking at new ways to view and score outcomes.[6] Public libraries, with limited resources of staff and time, could still create unbundled MOOCs—smaller, shorter lessons that, when combined, total a full course. Busy patrons plus busy librarians still can equal quality learning opportunities.

The above may seem daunting to some or far from the library's mission. Many of the folks in our MOOC have been confronting their own ideas of what it means to be a learner in a new and sometimes unsettling landscape. I'm here to learn, one participant told me, "and figure out how I might play a role in MOOCs on my campus."

I'm pleased and proud of the San José State University LIS students and student volunteers from other library schools who worked with co-instructor Kyle Jones and me on #hyperlibMOOC.[7] Dubbed "participatory learning guides," they helped oversee what we called "homerooms" of 35 to 40 students. The guides answered questions, troubleshot technical issues, and participated in leading the community of learners through our content modules and monitoring their activity in homeroom and the larger course environments or learner-created "tribe" spaces. The experience they gained will fit perfectly into the future skill sets needed for the scenarios above. Across all types of libraries, the librarian as community learning connector and collaborator might support learners on platforms that offer endless opportunities.

NOTES

1. Institute of Museum and Library Services, University of Washington Technology & Social Change Group, International City/County Management Association, *Building Digital Communities* (Washington, DC: Institute of Museum and Library Services, 2012), 1, https://www.imls.gov/assets/1/AssetManager/BuildingDigitalCommunities.pdf.
2. Ibid.
3. "Library You," Escondido Public Library, https://libraryyou.escondido.org.
4. Glenn Drexhage, "LOOCing into the Future of Digital Learning," *UBC News*, October 30, 2013, http://news.ubc.ca/2013/10/30/loocing-into-the-future-of-digital-learning/.
5. Brian Mathews, "Curating Learning Experiences: A Future Role for Librarians?" *The Chronicle for Higher Education*, September 5, 2013, http://chronicle.com/blognetwork/theubiquitouslibrarian/2013/09/05/curating-learning-experiences-a-future-role-for-librarians/.
6. Jeff Jarvis and Leo Laporte, "What's Italian for MMOC?" *This Week in Google: Episode 215* (September 11, 2013), television, https://twit.tv/shows/this-week-in-google/episodes/215.
7. "The Hyperlinked Library MOOC: An Overview of Research & Findings (So Far)," SLIS Colloquium Series, San José State University, http://ischool.sjsu.edu/about/multimedia-content/videos/hyperlinked-library-mooc-overview-research-findings-so-far.

LEARNING EVERYWHERE

AS I ALWAYS say, the annual *Horizon Report* is a valuable guide for LIS professors and librarians to review and even preview emerging technologies and trends. The 2012 report was no exception. It identified "key drivers of educational technology adoptions for the period 2012 through 2017."[1] These can enhance both LIS pedagogy and library service.

For example, "The world of work is increasingly collaborative, driving changes in the way student projects are structured."[2] Think back to your own library school experience. Remember the dreaded group project? There always seemed to be one student who hadn't done his assigned tasks, leaving conscientious group members scrambling to fill in the gaps as deadlines loomed. Now, my students use Dropbox to cloud-share documents, Google Docs for group collaboration, and Skype for meetings.

But it's not just technology, it's about working with others. The report notes, "Students are increasingly evaluated . . . on the success of the group dynamic," as well as the outcome.[3] This might involve peer evaluation and self-reflection in addition to review of the group's work.

The same expectations can and should apply in our libraries. Employing cloud services, open-sharing platforms such as blogs or wikis, and a high level of transparency strengthens collaboration among work groups and teams, since the process and outcomes are available for all to review. Performance evaluations can include analysis of work within these environments and the level of collaboration demonstrated. Team members might review one another's work as well as the work of the project leader. Extend the practice to administration. How might front-liners and managers evaluate those in charge?

Add to the mix another trend from the report: "There is a new emphasis in the classroom on more challenge-based and active learning."[4] Projects should not be passive "what if" endeavors. Jill Hurst-Wahl, associate professor of practice in Syracuse University's School of Information Studies, New York, told me her students embark on a "semester-long team assignment working with host librarians to create plans for new library services."

PRACTICING WHAT I PREACH

I've recently taught a new class based on Mezirow's concepts of transformative learning, the work of Char Booth in the arena of user instruction, and the Learning 2.0 model.[5] This is new and exciting territory for me, similar to Hurst-Wahl's. We worked with consultant Polly-Alida Farrington, who teamed up three groups of my students with two libraries and a school library consortium in New York state. Over the course of our fifteen-week semester, each group adapted, designed, and ran a "mini-23 Things" for its assigned organization.

It was a fun, chaotic, and messy experience. In our weekly group chats online, the mantra has become "Learn by doing." Real-world messiness offers a level of experience unmatched by classroom activities. This high-tech/high-touch experience set the students on course for getting jobs and taking on future projects. I am always interested to know about other LIS professors who are partnering with those in practice to go beyond prototypes and fictional creations.

PLACE-BASED NO MORE

Another trend states, "People expect to be able to work, learn, and study whenever and wherever they want to."[6] Lately, I've heard the term *place-based* as a descriptor for many of the limitations that confront both students and library users. How many of your administrative processes require people to visit your location? How many could be accomplished via the web or mobile technology? Delivering learning opportunities and access to collections to mobile users seamlessly and without barriers is a positive response to this trend.

Recently, I exchanged e-mails with a university library that has a unique artifact from a songwriter in its special collections. Teasingly, one page of lyrics is digitized and showcased on its website. The rest is only available if I travel to this distant institution. No seamless delivery there. The school cited concerns about "preservation and copyright" as reasons why I could not access these documents digitally. Really?

The trend "Education paradigms are shifting to include online learning, hybrid learning, and collaborative models" also describes the move from place-based learning and information access.[7] These ideas for change are synthesized in what Henry Jenkins calls "connected learning."[8] Jenkins, professor of communication, journalism, and cinematic arts at the University of Southern California, offers principles of connected learning that illustrate how far we've come and where we might be going: a shared purpose between learners and peers, a production-centered focus on creation and curation of things, and an openly networked atmosphere in which to work and learn.

Providing opportunities to gain knowledge—either formally within networked courses delivered across multiple channels by the university, or via services, collections, and access made seamless and available to anyone wherever they may be—is key for both LIS professors and librarians.

NOTES

1. Larry Johnson, S. Adams, and M. Cummins, *NMC Horizon Report: 2012 Higher Education Edition* (Austin, TX: New Media Consortium, 2012), 4, www.nmc.org/pdf/2012-horizon-report-HE.pdf.
2. Ibid.
3. Ibid.
4. Ibid., 5.
5. Jack Mezirow, *Transformative Dimensions of Adult Learning* (San Francisco: Jossey-Bass, 1991); Char Booth. *Reflective Teaching, Effective Learning: Instructional Literacy for Library Educators* (Chicago: American Library Association, 2011).
6. Johnson, Adams, and Cummins, *NMC Horizon Report: 2012 Higher Education Edition*, 4, www.nmc.org/pdf/2012-horizon-report-HE.pdf.
7. Ibid.
8. Henry Jenkins, "Connected Learning: Reimagining the Experience of Education in the Information Age," *Confessions of an Aca-Fan: The Official Weblog of Henry Jenkins,* March 1, 2012, http://henryjenkins.org/2012/03/connected_learning_a_new_parad.html.

LIBRARY AS CLASSROOM

READING THE *Horizon Report* for 2014, I was inspired as usual by the work of EDUCAUSE and the New Media Consortium.[1] A new framework for presenting challenges and trends accelerating technology adoption and the key technologies for higher education makes the report even more useful for anyone and everyone involved in teaching and learning.

I've often argued for public libraries to use this report as a means for trend-spotting and planning, and today it is more relevant than ever. As our colleagues in academic libraries embrace the idea that students are creators more than consumers and welcome an influx of hybrid and online learning opportunities, they are not alone. Related courses are impacting public library customers in the form of makerspaces, self-publishing, and library-led lifelong learning options both formal and self-directed. As a result, those guiding technology and training programs in the public sector would also benefit from a deep dive into this document.

CREATIVE CLASSROOMS

The Elements of the Creative Classroom Research Model, developed by the European Commission Institute for Prospective Technological Studies and highlighted as part of the *Horizon Report*'s methodology, represent the catalysts and potential for new models of instruction.[2] The team's report defines creative classrooms as "learning environments that fully embed the potential of [information and communications technology] to innovate and modernize learning and teaching practices," and the term *classrooms* is used "in its widest sense as including all types of learning environments, in formal and informal settings."[3]

The 2014 *Horizon Report* includes a graphic that depicts the model.[4] Radiating out from a center focused on innovative pedagogical practices are eight interconnected key areas, including curriculum, learning practices, leadership, and infrastructure. Further, twenty-eight building blocks are identified around the outer circle, supporting each of the key areas. These include themes I write about often: innovation management; learning by play, exploration, and creation; emotional intelligence; meaningful activities; and networking with the real world.

A NEW KIND OF CLASSROOM

I'd argue that our libraries of all kinds also serve as creative classrooms, supporting learners by employing the building blocks mentioned above. There are examples from academic, public, and K–12 library spaces where community-learning spaces help people achieve, game-focused initiatives make the library a laboratory for exploration, and creation zones with requisite digital and 3-D hardware allow people to build things. There are potentially endless opportunities to connect virtually with people worldwide.

A recent example provides a glimpse of a life-changing use of a 3-D printer. You may have seen it on the national news. A teenager printed a prosthetic hand for a young boy at Johnson County Libraries, Kansas.[5] This is the "learning by creating" highlighted in the model and so much more. Other areas of the model came into play that afforded this unique opportunity for such a caring act to occur. Leaders at Johnson County, a library I follow closely, are well versed in innovation management and social entrepreneurship and the recognition that offering learning events can bring people together. Consider another program they implemented, the "Books and Butchers" program, which featured a local butcher and "an actual pig, with actual knives and actual cutting of actual meat."[6] Sean Casserly, director of the library, told me the meeting room was packed and the crowd was mesmerized by the butcher's skill and his discussion of local food and humanely raised meat.

LET IMAGINATIONS PLAY

The model calls for constant monitoring of program quality, innovative timetables that enable flexible programs and services to evolve without bureaucratic barriers, and a focus on fresh services. The library as classroom requires inspired and insightful management that can do those things and more. The library as classroom also requires well-trained, user-focused staff who understand how people of all ages can learn socially. Art programs, do-it-yourself tinkering, locally sourced expert forums, and local open online courses are all part of this curriculum.

In *A New Culture of Learning*, authors Douglas Thomas and John Seely Brown write, "Where imaginations play, learning happens."[7] This could and should define our services for now and in the future. The library as creative classroom means we approach the learning opportunities we create with thought, user-directed planning, and insights from research. This classroom may include physical spaces for instruction and discovery as well as online, multiscale platforms aimed at social learning and participation.

NOTES

1. Larry Johnson, S. Adams Becker, V. Estrada, and A. Freeman, *NMC Horizon Report: 2014 Higher Education Edition* (Austin, TX: New Media Consortium, 2014), www.nmc.org/pdf/2014-nmc-horizon-report-he-EN.pdf.
2. Stefani Bocconi, Panagiotis G. Kampylis, and Yves Punie, "Innovative Learning: Key Elements for Developing Creative Classrooms in Europe," Joint Research Centre–Institute for Prospective Technological Studies, European Commission (Luxembourg: Publications Office of the European Union, 2012), http://ftp.jrc.es/EURdoc/JRC72278.pdf.
3. Ibid., 4.
4. Johnson, Adams Becker, Estrada, and Freeman. *NMC Horizon Report: 2014 Higher Education Edition*, 4, www.nmc.org/pdf/2014-nmc-horizon-report-he-EN.pdf.
5. Mara Rose Williams, "Kansas Teen Uses 3-D Printer to Make Hand for Boy," *The Kansas City Star*, January 31, 2014, www.kansascity.com/news/local/article337980/Kansas-teen-uses-3-D-printer-to-make-hand-for-boy.html.
6. "Books and Butchers," Johnson County Libraries, www.jocolibrary.org/newsroom/books-and-butchers.
7. Douglas Thomas and John Seely Brown, *A New Culture of Learning: Cultivating the Imagination for a World of Constant Change* (Lexington, KY: Create Space, 2011), 102.

A GENIUS IDEA

THE LIBRARIAN SHAMING Tumblr highlights anonymous "confessions" from our field.[1] Some are humorous, some shocking. Some will make you think and maybe reconsider assumptions. This shameful confession perked me up when I discovered it: "I want to replace all librarians with tech people with great customer service skills and teaching ability. I want the library to have its own Genius Bar."

While a bit narrow in focus, this statement resonates on an instinctive level with me as an LIS educator. In some ways, it makes perfect sense: many library folk, myself included, have stressed that the teaching function of our evolving service-oriented duties will only grow over time. We need to be broader.

But before we do that, let's consider this suggestion. Perhaps the person who shared this dramatic wish has only experienced one library environment, rife with stagnant folks who refuse to learn or try new things. Maybe the confessor is burnt out on working at the service desk, providing less than great service. Possibly that staffer has simply checked out. Maybe the clientele of this particular library have changed of late. They look to the library not for "reference-y"-style help but assistance with mobile devices or other technological needs. Had the shaming poster witnessed one too many requests for help going unanswered?

ADDING A STROKE OF GENIUS

Let's unpack this sweeping suggestion for improving libraries further. What of teaching ability? I advise my students to make sure they take courses in user instruction and technology, no matter where they want to work. Delivering instruction should be a part of every professional's skill set: in a training room, across the desk, in the stacks, on the fly. Maybe it's time to add creating a short training session or learning module to the interview process for all librarians, not just those in colleges or schools.

Borrowed from Apple, the Genius Bar concept applied to libraries is not new, but it's a welcome addition to many library settings.[2]

David Weinberger, in "The Library as Platform," notes that the Genius Bar might be one of many channels for users to interact with librarians.[3] Libraries such as DOK Delft and others have tried various permutations of walk-in tech assistance.

John Pappas, when branch director at the Primos Branch of the Upper Darby Free Library, Pennsylvania, told me, "I have drop-in digital device clinics once a week for four hours at my branch." Kenley Neufeld, when library director at Santa Barbara City College, California, countered my call for Genius Bar examples with, "Yes, it's called the reference desk. No appointment necessary." Touché, Kenley. The libraries that have rebranded their reference desks— I'm reminded of the "Ask Here" signage at the Allen County Public Library, Fort Wayne, Indiana—have already discovered that people are attracted to such non-library phrasing.

WHO COULD IT BE NOW?

So in the vision shared at Librarian Shaming, librarians are out the door and tech-savvy, user-focused, service-driven folks would replace them. Who could that be? More librarians? Better librarians? The statement, while shocking and a bit frustrating, may be rooted in truth. Isn't this the evolution we are seeing in libraries?

If you've done any future visioning or strategic planning of late, haven't the conversations turned to more active, technologically enhanced spaces and services? More classes, more space for working with creation tools, more time spent showing people how things work? Is this what people are asking for? Consider this option in our evolution: we might continue to hire degreed librarians who will be managing projects and guiding services but also some very specialized folks—maybe they'll have a library degree, maybe they won't— who work with users and new technology in these collaborative spaces.

HOW TO TEACH TECH LEADERS

LIS curricula must keep up as well. At San José State University's School of Library and Information Science, we're offering a new class entitled "Production of Knowledge and Content in Libraries," taught by Monica Harris, deputy director, Schaumburg Township District Library, Illinois. Her syllabus, focused on participation and creativity, runs from digital creation spaces to the maker movement to a module called the "Importance of Informal Learning." Another unit highlights robotics and electronics: Arduino, Sensors, and LEGO.

When I taught the Hyperlinked Library, discussion turned to the changing roles of librarians in the evolving library. One student responded to an early lecture, asking, "Do we even need librarians?" Exploring similar ideas to the post above, the student continued, "To me, a professional who advocates for people to learn, access, and create knowledge on their terms sounds like a pretty respectable calling." I think so, too. The post that inspired this column isn't a diatribe, steeped in negativity. It's a call to arms to keep thinking strategically about our spaces, services, and learning.

NOTES

1. Librarian Shaming Tumblr, http://librarian-shaming.tumblr.com.
2. "Genius Bar," Apple, www.apple.com/retail/geniusbar/.
3. David Weinberger, "Library as Platform," *Library Journal,* September 4, 2012, http://lj.libraryjournal.com/2012/09/future-of-libraries/by-david-weinberger/#_.

ROOM TO GROW

A FEW YEARS ago at the ALA's Annual Conference in Anaheim, California, I had dinner with librarians from three large universities. The conversation turned to something they had in common: they were all moving print book collections at their respective institutions off-site to make room for student spaces. Back then, this was a big deal, and these administrators met with opposition and angst from their constituents.

I still hear rumblings in the academy that these changes to what might be perceived as traditional libraries are sometimes met with dissent and discord. Library spaces morphing into "collaboratories" filled with creation tools and collections existing off-site or in the cloud can be disruptive forces, likened to chaos. Yet this trend isn't reversing any time soon; recent research supports a much different landscape in 2015: academic library spaces are learner-centered and evolving just like our skills, tools, and mind-sets.

STUDIES SEE SPACE SHIFTS

The 2015 *Horizon Report* recently came out, and one of many salient "Key Trends Accelerating Technology Adoption in Higher Education" resonates with me as I reflect on evolving spaces for learning.[1] A notable trend that will drive technology adoption in higher education for the next one to two years is "Redesigning Learning Spaces." The report states that "academic libraries across the globe are seeing a flurry of activity as their informal learning spaces are being reimagined to take advantage of the emerging maker movement," and "the physical layout of university libraries is currently being redrawn so that row upon row of stacks containing books that have not been touched in decades can be archived to make room for more productive use of floor space."[2]

A study I helped coauthor in *First Monday* also details insights and solutions to the challenges of supporting higher education in libraries and information technology.[3] Survey respondents noted that library spaces are being transformed, becoming "salons" and places for multiple groups to collaborate as collections go digital. Implementing new standards, evaluating services, and focusing on adapting roles to meet learner and researcher needs were all part of the response to the disruptive forces confronting our institutions. One respondent was "creating a learning organization academy" to help their institution change.

The Ithaka S+R Library Survey for 2013 also supports these changes, stating, "There is ample evidence that library directors' opinions about print collections are changing over time; a large majority of respondents agreed with the idea that building local physical collections is less important than it used to be."[4] Mal Booth, a librarian from the University of Technology Sydney, agrees: "Smart library spaces are now not about accessing print collections, they're becoming more about harnessing new/available technologies to create, mix, mash, and edit new forms of knowledge and culture." It's a given: libraries should not be seen primarily as book storage facilities. Library spaces are much more valuable than that.

STILL ROOM FOR LIBRARIANS

If our academic libraries could soon be landscapes of computer access to collections and maker-style spaces, where does one of the most valuable parts of the library—the librarian—fit? In "Why Don't Students Ask Librarians for Help? Undergraduate Help-Seeking Behavior in Three Academic Libraries," part of the Ethnographic Research in Illinois Academic Libraries Project, authors Susan Miller and Nancy Murillo present findings that students may not go to librarians for help, instead turning to people they know: professors, peers, family, and friends.[5] The role of the librarian is muddy at best for most undergrads. This begs the question: How successful will these learning spaces be if students are afraid of librarian intervention? Are they going to be self-directed explorers? Maybe in library facilities designed to enable collaboration, librarians are getting out of the way and letting students work together, providing tools and instruction needed to enable success.

I'm encouraged by the ideas of Keith Webster, dean of university libraries at Carnegie Mellon University, who shares his thoughts on the twenty-first-century library at his blog *Library of the Future*. Webster notes that as faculty and students meet their needs online, library service must be delivered outside the library. "The librarian must interact with his or her clients wherever they are: in laboratories, clinics, offices, and lecture theaters."[6] This involves one of the most challenging issues we face: how do we advocate for ourselves and the roles we play in research, knowledge creation, and technology use? Webster asks, "How do we share that message?"

Librarians have long used and refined service models, from building collections to planning spaces. Recent research tells us that as newer methods emerge to access and store knowledge, library space can become even more user-focused and allow explorations of the world's knowledge, with room to grow.

NOTES

1. Larry Johnson, S. Adams Becker, V. Estrada, and A. Freeman, *NMC Horizon Report: 2015 Higher Education Edition* (Austin, TX: New Media Consortium, 2015), 6, http://cdn.nmc.org/media/2015-nmc-horizon-report-HE-EN.pdf.
2. Ibid., 18.
3. Michael Stephens, David Wedaman, Ellen Freeman, Alison Hicks, Gail Matthews-DeNatale, Diane Wahl, and Lisa Spiro, "Academic 15: Evaluating Library and IT Staff Responses to Disruption and Change in Higher Education," *First Monday* 19, no. 5 (2015), http://firstmonday.org/ojs/index.php/fm/article/view/4635/3878.
4. Matthew P. Long and Roger C. Schonfeld, "Ithaka S+R US Library Survey 2013," Ithaka S+R, March 11, 2014, www.sr.ithaka.org/wp-content/uploads/2015/08/SR_LibraryReport_20140310_0.pdf.
5. Susan Miller and Nancy Murillo, "Why Don't Students Ask Librarians for Help? Undergraduate Help-Seeking Behavior in Three Academic Libraries," in *College Libraries and Student Culture: What We Now Know* (Chicago: American Library Association, 2012), 49–70.
6. Keith Webster, "In the Beginning," *Library of the Future*, March 13, 2015, www.libraryofthefuture.org/blog/2015/3/13/in-the-beginning.

LESSONS FROM LEARNING 2.0

IT HAS BEEN a few years since Helene Blowers and the staff at the Charlotte Mecklenburg Library, North Carolina, debuted Learning 2.0—a self-directed exploration of emerging technologies shared via a Creative Commons license.[1] The program has been touted as transformational for libraries—a method of moving libraries forward into a future of twenty-first-century innovation. The tools may change—many of the more recent programs have added Twitter and Facebook—but the goals remain the same: library staff should explore, work together to play with emerging technology, reflect on the usefulness of those tools, and examine their application in information settings.

With Warren Cheetham, coordinator for information and digital services at CityLibraries in Townsville, Queensland, Australia, I've been mining the data from my Learning 2.0 research project, sponsored by CAVAL, an Australian nonprofit established to provide library services to libraries in Australia, New Zealand, and Asia.[2] Surveys of program leaders and participants and on-site focus groups have yielded valuable insights into the aftermath of Learning 2.0, including an emphasis on continuing the learning and approach after the program concludes.

LEARNING 2.0 OUTCOMES

Here's what library staff had to say in the surveys: participants adopted Web 2.0 tools into both their professional and personal lives. They found that the new knowledge they gained had a practical application to their work. Noting the usefulness specifically of RSS feeds, respondents reported increased use of the tools to enhance ongoing professional development as well as personal pursuits.

Participants were more confident about using new technology and more open to exploring emerging technology. Library staff who took our surveys or participated in focus groups were quick to say they felt more knowledgeable attending meetings focused on emerging technologies and that they could better understand "IT speak."

Participants felt equally valued as learners in the Learning 2.0 program. One cornerstone of the program has been offering it to all employees, not just professional staff or administration. This leveling of the playing field is perceived as beneficial to all staff, promoting feelings of inclusion. Some directors of organizations with tight budgets might balk at giving front-line clerks extra training. The data shows that everyone benefits from this experience.

Other results from the data include:

- Noncompletion does not imply program failure. Those who did not finish still reported success and confidence gained.
- Impact is mainly personal, but organizational changes may follow. Staff reported successful outreach to local government and users about new tools.

SUSTAINING THE LEARNING

Some survey respondents expressed concerns that post-program, everything returned to the status quo in their institutions.[3] Fostering a true "learning organization" is not done in just 10 or 12 weeks, but the seeds planted by Learning 2.0 can prove fruitful if nurtured. Libraries that have offered Learning 2.0 are best served by continued exploration via more "things" offered monthly.

In their recent book, *A New Culture of Learning*, Douglas Thomas and John Seely Brown explore similar concepts and the importance of continuous learning.[4] The parallels to the original Learning 2.0 model are striking. The book is based on several assumptions about our new normal, for example, that as the world changes ever more rapidly, so must our skill sets. Planning for ongoing organizational learning for staff may seem like just "one more thing" in our stressed environments, but without backing and emphasis from library leaders, exploration and innovation may wane.

The library should serve as a hub for sustaining a culture of learning around technology and research using variations on the model. Extending the program to users or shifting focus from technologies to other areas of learning and reflection is a natural progression. The public "Looking at 2.0" program at the State Library of Queensland continues to engage users with topics and award prizes.[5] Consider new audiences as well, such as Research 2.0, a program created for researchers at the Imperial College in the United Kingdom.[6]

Beginning this learner's journey in library school should be a given. The role of the LIS instructor becomes guide, not keeper of knowledge. Students could also set aside part of their schoolwork time to explore beyond class content. "Follow your curiosity" is my answer when students ask me what emerging ideas and tech they should focus on. This emphasis on learning will carry our graduates forward into their positions.

NOTES

1. Learning 2.0, http://plcmclearning.blogspot.com.
2. Michael Stephens and Warren Cheetham, "Benefits and Results of Learning 2.0: A Case Study of CityLibrariesLearning—discover*play*connect," *The Australian Library Journal* 61, no. 1 (2012): 6–15.

3. Ibid.
4. Douglas Thomas and John Seely Brown, *A New Culture of Learning: Cultivating the Imagination for a World of Constant Change* (Lexington, KY: Create Space, 2011), 102.
5. State Library of Queensland, http://learning.slq.qld.gov.au.
6. Janet Corcoran, "Blogs, Twitter, Wikis, and Other Web-Based Tools— Programme for Researchers," *Imperial College News,* May 9, 2013, www3. imperial.ac.uk/newsandeventspggrp/imperialcollege/administration/library/ newssummary/news_9-5-2013-9-52-15.

LESSONS FROM #HYPERLIBMOOC

TRACING THE EVOLUTION of professional development programs in libraries has been an interest of mine since I was an Internet trainer in the mid-1990s. Conferences and daylong workshops were the way we shared and learned back then, along with the occasional teleconference or visiting speaker. Webinars paved the way for on-line channels to deliver development. Learning 2.0 changed the landscape even further in 2006.

With my co-instructor Kyle Jones, who is currently working toward his doctorate at the University of Wisconsin-Madison's iSchool, I am mining the survey data from the Hyperlinked Library MOOC that we taught several semesters ago for over three hundred LIS professionals. With support from the San José State University School of Library and Information Science, feedback on the broad professional development opportunity we offered is providing some unique views of how models of online learning for library staff continue to evolve.

MOOC OUTCOMES

The post-MOOC survey data is full of rich insights and ideas for future offerings. Kyle and I are working on journal articles that explore participants' sense of community, perceptions of success, and suggestions for refining the MOOC for the future, as well as the bespoke learning environment built on WordPress and BuddyPress.

We asked participants what their major takeaways were, and the results are most interesting. They reported, in order of frequency, that they learned about new ideas, knowledge, and trends; discovered that they are able to learn, collaborate, and discuss and exchange ideas with others in evolving networks and with those beyond their individual library environments; and gained perspectives about themselves through personal reflection on their learning styles, professional practices, and the ways they view the world. Others came away with inspiration, energy, and excitement about our field, as well as new technological skills.

A LIFE OF ITS OWN

One of the most intriguing aspects of the course has been the life of #hyperlibMOOC outside of what Kyle and I created. Throughout the course, participants extended the learning to Twitter, GoodReads, and other social sites. As the course concluded, a core, most active group of #hyperlibMOOC folks spun off a blog of their own and started an "alumni" group on Facebook.

At an ALA Midwinter Meeting, I met up with MOOC student Amy Paget, a librarian at the Tippecanoe County Public Library, Indiana. Amy was handing out ribbons for name tags emblazoned with "Hyperlinked Library Alumni." Gestures such as this touch my heart deeply.

LIBRARIAN'S ROLES

Kyle and I wrote a paper for the proceedings of the 16th Distance Library Services Conference this month in Denver based on this post-MOOC survey question: "Reflecting on your MOOC experience, what roles do you think librarians might play within MOOCs?"[1] The identified roles include:

Guide

Rarely in the library, working on the go, from home or third place, or amid the MOOC community served, the librarian gives learners what they want and need, with an arsenal of technological tools.

Access Provider

Building, curating, and sharing resources to help learners wherever they may be, without the confines and barriers we're accustomed to. This librarian works with authors, scholars, and other content providers to make resources available as openly as possible. Contracts may include "MOOC clauses" for open access.

Creator

Librarians create large-scale, small-scale, or "just right" formalized courses for their constituents across a wide spectrum of topics and varying degrees of focus.

Instructor

New platforms and methods of offering learning can extend how librarians instruct those they serve. These new environments will encourage librarians to capture and curate more knowledge and package it for anywhere, anytime learning.

LESSONS LEARNED

As travel and conference budgets continue to shrink, I hope there will be more opportunities for open, sweeping, global learning such as #hyperlibMOOC. Going forward, an LIS professional might continue to use such platforms to keep current with emerging ideas and issues in librarianship as well as specific subjects of interest. The Library Advocacy Unshushed MOOC, co-taught by Wendy Newman from the University of Toronto, also focuses on a timely and important area of librarianship.[2] I look forward to a rich set of communities offering lifelong learning for LIS professionals.

NOTES

1. Michael Stephens and Kyle M. Jones, "Emerging Roles: Key Insights from Librarians in a Massive Open Online Course," 16th Distance Library Services Conferences, April 23, 2014, http://libguides.cmich.edu/dls2014/ataglance/papers.
2. Library Advocacy Unshushed MOOC, https://www.edx.org/course/library-advocacy-unshushed-university-torontox-la101x#.VLBbWGMpcin.

LEARNING TO LEARN

"BEING ADAPTABLE IN a flat world, knowing how to 'learn how to learn,' will be one of the most important assets any worker can have, because job churn will come faster, because innovation will happen faster," writes Thomas Friedman in *The World Is Flat 3.0*.[1] I've invoked this "learn to learn" mantra before, but recent shifts in the opportunities for librarians and library staff to learn have brought me back to it.

I've presented at a fair share of library staff development days. I enjoy them. Staff come together, usually with the library closed, for updates from the director, a speaker or two, a chance to learn something new. These sessions might be focused on LIS—I usually talk about evolving library services and socio-technological change—or centered on personal improvement and include such content as yoga demonstrations, stress reduction techniques, or healthy cooking. These are all good things, especially if used as a starting point for "healthy library" initiatives or a future-focused strategic planning year. Sometimes, though, I worry that there's great excitement about learning during staff day that doesn't last. Many staff days get folks energized, but then the excitement dies down the following week.

LEARNING MOMENTUM

How might staff development days evolve? I was impressed with the activities at the Highland Park Public Library, Illinois, when I spoke at the library's staff day a couple of years ago. Staff participated in a live, hands-on "passport to technology" program. Stations around the building offered staff members the chance to try out new devices and new web services offered by the library. The Best Buy Geek Squad was in attendance as well, offering encounters with popular and best-selling consumer tech. At each station, employees received a stamp in a passport. Filling all the blanks entered each person into a number of drawings for e-readers. It was Learning 2.0 with a hands-on twist.

I'd argue for continuing staff development days, but I'd also urge administrators to promote a culture of learning all year long. At a workshop recently in Alberta, Canada, an administrator asked me how to incorporate all the new ideas and services we were talking about into practice. "How do we balance it all out?" she asked.

I suggested two strategies, one for management and one for staff. For administrators: mandate weekly time for each staff member to explore something new related to their jobs. It might be a social tool, a web service, or simply distraction-free time to read a few articles or a book. Reports on learning progress should figure into performance evaluations and monthly meetings.

Staff should then make good use of the time they're given. They could start an exploration blog to chart progress and post each week as part of the activity. They could formalize reading an important work, such as David Weinberger's *Everything Is Miscellaneous* or Chris Anderson's new book *Makers*.[2] Investigate the great things the Nebraska Library Commission has done with the Learning 2.0 model: offering supplemental technologies to explore and posts on important written works that participants can receive continuing education credits for reading.[3]

Another strategy might involve participating in a new, no-cost online learning opportunity like the "23 Mobile Things," created by Jan Holmquist in Denmark, along with Mylee Joseph and Kathryn

Barwick from Australia.[4] This online program extends a new twist on the Learning 2.0 model: 23 mobile applications for library staff to explore as a means to understand how people are using apps. Participants can reflect and consider the tools for use within the library. Take a look at a group of more than six hundred Australian and New Zealander self-organized library staff who have already adapted the program for more inspiration.[5]

LEARNING MEETS THE ROAD

I've researched Learning 2.0-style programs and the impact of such staff education since 2008. A recent study with a group of Chicago-area libraries further illuminates exemplary practice for creating a culture of learning in your organization, including the notion that all staff should participate in educational opportunities, not just librarians or managers; program creators should focus learning programs on practical implementations of new tools and services; and "learning champion" staff members should be designated as support throughout the program in each department or service area.[6]

A mantra I use in my talks and in my classes is "Learn Always." I'm impressed with some of the grassroots learning activities I've witnessed of late that give library staff low-cost, active learning opportunities. If libraries call themselves learning organizations, setting time aside for staff to explore and reflect is mandatory.

NOTES

1. Thomas Friedman, *The World Is Flat 3.0: A Brief History of the Twenty-First Century* (New York: Picador, 2007).
2. David Weinberger, *Everything Is Miscellaneous: The Power of the New Digital Disorder* (New York: Times Books, 2007); Chris Anderson, *Makers: The New Industrial Revolution* (New York: Crown Business, 2012).
3. Nebraska Library Commission, http://nlcblogs.nebraska.gov/nelearns/.
4. 23 Mobile Things, http://23mobilethings.net/wpress/.
5. 23 Mobile Things, https://anz23mobilethings.wordpress.com.
6. Michael Stephens, "Exemplary Practice for Learning 2.0: Based on a Cumulative Analysis for the Value and Effect of '23 Things' Programs in Libraries," *Reference and User Services Quarterly* 53, no. 2 (2013).

BIBLIOGRAPHY

Anderson, Chris. *Makers: The New Industrial Revolution*. New York: Crown Business, 2012.

Bilton, Nick. *I Live in the Future and Here's How It Works: Why Your World, Work, and Brain Are Being Creatively Disrupted*. New York: Crown Business, 2011.

Block, Peter. *Community: The Structure of Belonging*. Oakland, CA: Berrett-Koehler, 2009.

Booth, Char. *Reflective Teaching, Effective Learning: Instructional Literacy for Library Educators*. Chicago: American Library Association, 2011.

Boyd, Danah. *It's Complicated: The Social Lives of Networked Teens*. New Haven, CT: Yale University Press, 2014.

Cain, Susan. *Quiet: The Power of Introverts in a World That Can't Stop Talking*. New York: Crown Publishing, 2012.

Clyde, Laurel Ann. *Weblogs and Libraries*. Oxford: Chandos, 2004.

Friedman, Thomas. *The World Is Flat 3.0: A Brief History of the Twenty-First Century*. New York: Picador, 2007.

Godin, Seth. *Linchpin: Are You Indispensable? How to Drive Your Career and Create a Remarkable Future*. New York: Portfolio, 2010.

———. *Tribes: We Need You to Lead Us*. New York: Portfolio, 2008.

Grant, Carl A., and Kenneth M. Zeichner. "On Becoming a Reflective Teacher." In *Preparing for Reflective Teaching*. Boston: Allyn & Bacon, 1984.

Grazer, Brian, and Charles Fishman. *A Curious Mind: The Secret to a Bigger Life*. New York: Simon & Schuster, 2015.

Hiemstra, Roger. *Lifelong Learning*. 3rd ed. Fayetteville, NY: HiTree, 2002.

Ito, Mizuko. *Hanging Out, Messing Around, and Geeking Out: Kids Living and Learning with New Media*. Cambridge, MA: MIT Press, 2013.

Krznaric, Roman. *Empathy: Why It Matters, and How to Get It.* New York: TarcherPerigree, 2014.

Linkner, Josh. *Disciplined Dreaming: A Proven System to Drive Breakthrough Creativity.* San Francisco: Jossey-Bass, 2011.

Mezirow, Jack. *Transformative Dimensions of Adult Learning.* San Francisco: Jossey-Bass, 1991.

Pausch, Randy, and Jeffrey Zaslow. *The Last Lecture.* New York: Hyperion, 2008.

Pink, Daniel H. *A Whole New Mind: Why Right-Brainers Will Rule the Future.* New York: Penguin, 2006.

Powell, Lawrence Clark. *The Little Package: Pages on Literature and Landscape from a Traveling Bookman's Life.* Cleveland, OH: World Publishing, 1964.

Rifkin, Jeremy. *The Empathic Civilization.* New York: TarcherPerigree, 2009.

Shirky, Clay. *Cognitive Surplus: Creativity and Generosity in a Connected Age.* New York: Penguin, 2010.

————. *Here Comes Everybody: The Power of Organizing without Organizations.* New York: Penguin, 2008.

Sinek, Simon. *Start with Why: How Great Leaders Inspire Everyone to Take Action.* New York: Portfolio, 2011.

Standage, Tom. *Writing on the Wall: Social Media—The First 2,000 Years.* New York: Bloomsbury Publishing, 2013.

Thomas, Douglas, and John Seely Brown. *A New Culture of Learning: Cultivating the Imagination for a World of Constant Change.* Lexington, KY: Create Space, 2011.

Weinberger, David. *Everything Is Miscellaneous: The Power of the New Digital Disorder.* New York: Times Books, 2007.

INDEX